MW01594819

Hanzi Bu Mafan

Name _____

Class _____

ISBN-10: 1-946626-45-5
ISBN-13: 978-1-946626-45-5

Contents

My Character Picture for
Bù / bÚ   not/no

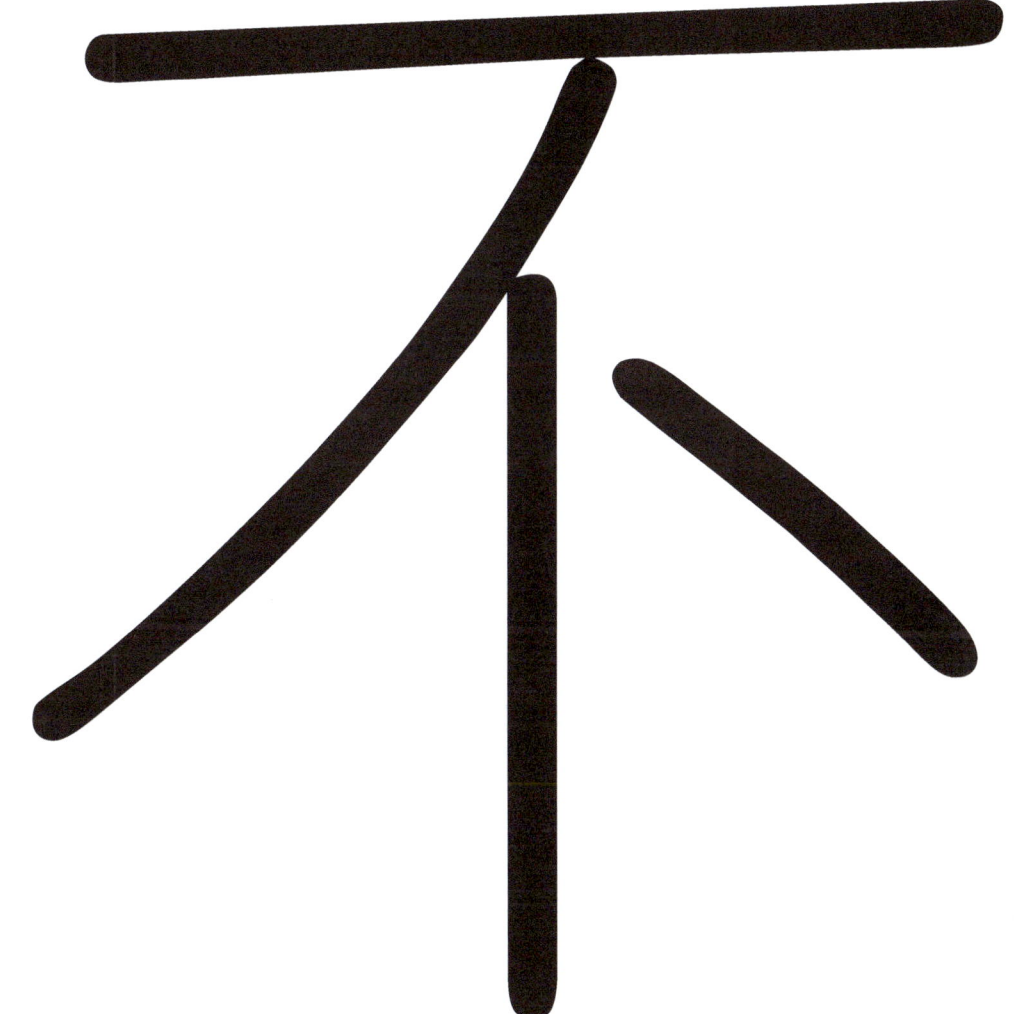

Describe your picture and write how you will remember what the character means and what it sounds like:

名字＿＿＿＿＿＿＿＿＿＿＿ ＿＿年 ＿＿月 ＿＿日

不

Simplified

Bù / bÚ

not / no

不

Traditional

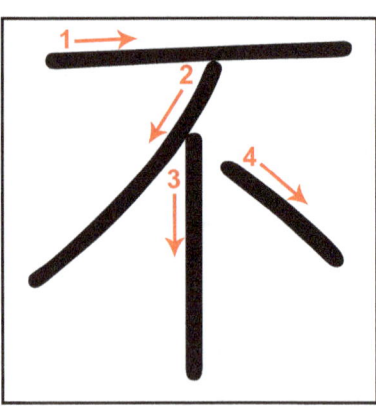

不好 Bùhǎo *bad*

不对 bÚDuì *wrong*

不是 bÚShì *it is not*

不要 bÚYào *don't! don't want*

不同 BùtónG *different*

Strokes: 4

Radical: 一 Yī 'one'

Pinyin: bù / bú

Practice writing this character using the stroke order shown above.
When you're finished, circle the one that you like the best.

不 不 不 不 不 不

2

My Character Picture for
CHĪ *eat*

Describe your picture and write how you will remember what the character means and what it sounds like:

吃
Simplified

CHĪ
eat

吃
Traditional

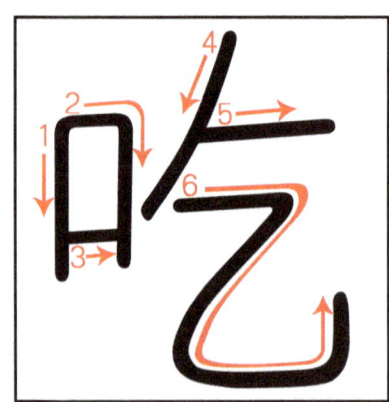

吃 CHĪ *eat*

吃饭 CHĪFàn *eat, have a meal*

好吃 hǎoCHĪ *good to eat, yummy*

吃饱了 CHĪbǎole* *eat one's fill*

吃素 CHĪSù *be a vegetarian*

Strokes: 6

Radical: 口 kǒu
'*mouth*'

Pinyin: chī

Practice writing this character using the stroke order shown above.
When you're finished, circle the one that you like the best.

My Character Picture for
Dàn   but/yet/still

Describe your picture and write how you will remember what the character means and what it sounds like:

但
Simplified

Dàn

but / yet / still

但
Traditional

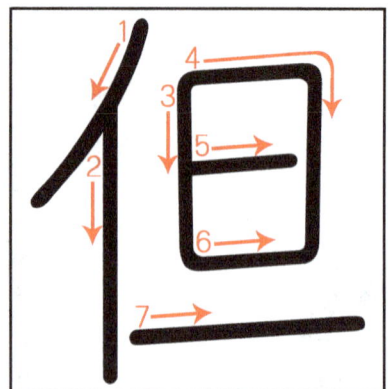

但是　DànShì　*but, however*

但愿　DànYuàn　*if only it were possible to…*

不但…而且　bÚDàn…éRqiě　*not only…but also*

Strokes: 7

Radical: 亻（人）réN　'*person*'

Pinyin: dàn

Practice writing this character using the stroke order shown above.
When you're finished, circle the one that you like the best.

但　但　但　但　但　但

但 但 但 **但** 但 但 但 但 但

My Character Picture for
Dào   path/method/way

Describe your picture and write how you will remember what the character means and what it sounds like:

_____

道

Simplified

Dào

path / method / way

道

Traditional

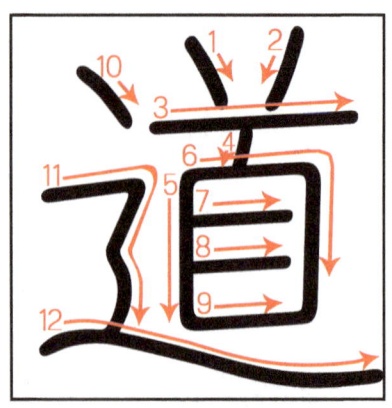

知道 ZHĪDào *knows*

不知道 BùZHĪDào *don't know*

道路 DàoLù *path*

难道 náNDào *is it possible*

人行道 réNxíNGDào *sidewalk*

Strokes: 12

Radical: 辶(辵)  Chuò *'walk'*

Pinyin: dào

Practice writing this character using the stroke order shown above.
When you're finished, circle the one that you like the best.

道 道 道 道 道 道

道 道 道 道 道 道 道

My Character Picture for

de* *(possessive particle)*

Describe your picture and write how you will remember what the character means and what it sounds like:

的
Simplified

de*
(possessive particle)

的
Traditional

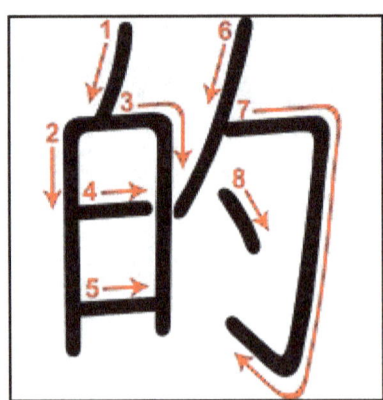

他的 TĀde* *his*

她的 TĀde* *hers*

我的 wǒde* *my, mine*

有的 yǒude* *some*

是的 Shìde* *as if, seem*

Strokes: 8

Radical: 白 báI 'white'

Pinyin: de

Practice writing this character using the stroke order shown above.
When you're finished, circle the one that you like the best.

的 的 的 的 的 的

的 的 的 的 的 的 的 的

My Character Picture for
Diàn   *electricity*

Describe your picture and write how you will remember what the character means and what it sounds like:

名字＿＿＿＿＿＿＿＿＿＿＿＿＿＿＿ ＿＿＿＿年 ＿＿＿月 ＿＿＿日

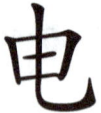

电 Diàn 電

Simplified — electricity — Traditional

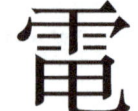

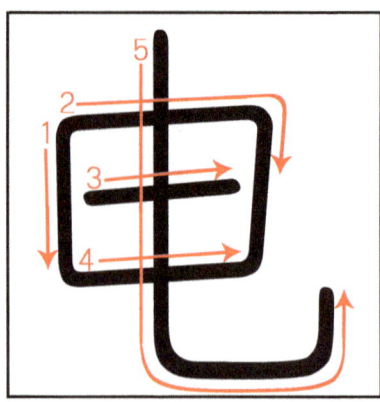

电影 Diànyǐng *movie*

电脑 Diànnǎo *computer*

电视 DiànShì *television*

电话 DiànHuà *telephone*

闪电 shǎnDiàn *lightning*

Strokes: 5

Radical: 田 tiáN *'field'*

Pinyin: diàn

Practice writing this character using the stroke order shown above.
When you're finished, circle the one that you like the best.

电	电	电	电	电	电

電 电 电 电 电 电 电 电 电

My Character Picture for
diǎn   *drop/spot*

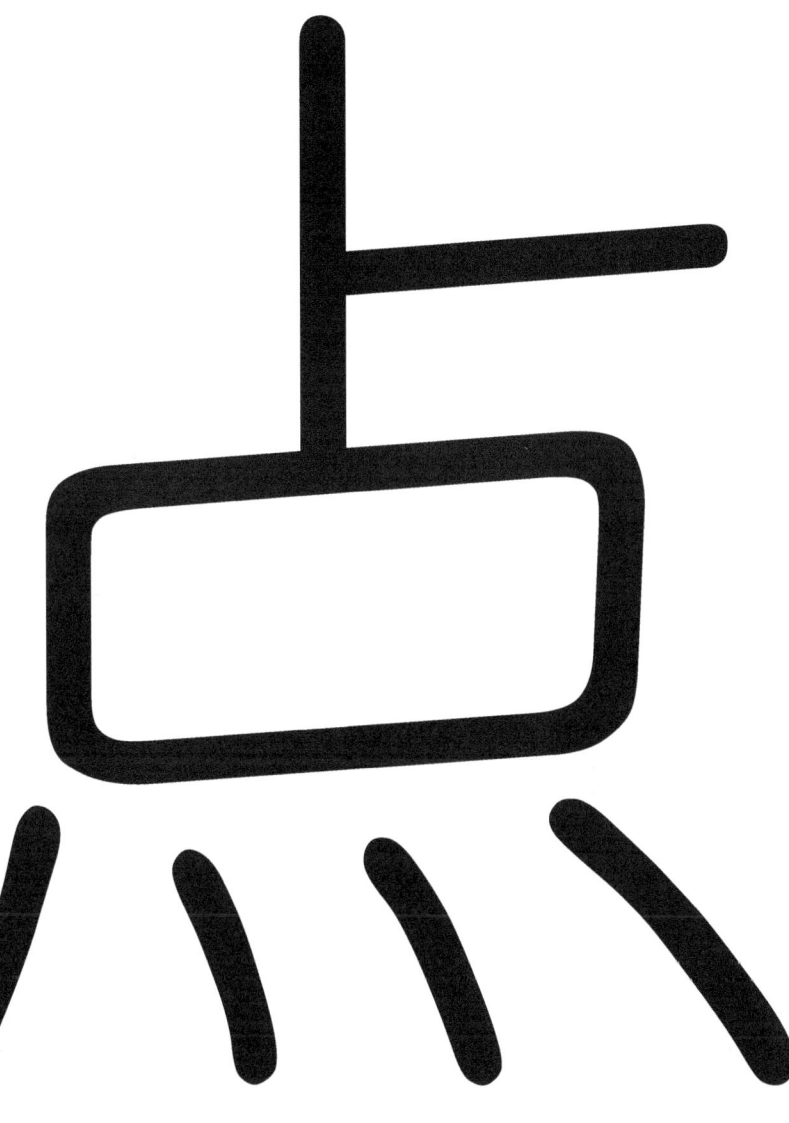

Describe your picture and write how you will remember what the character means and what it sounds like:

点

Simplified

diǎn

drop / spot

點

Traditional

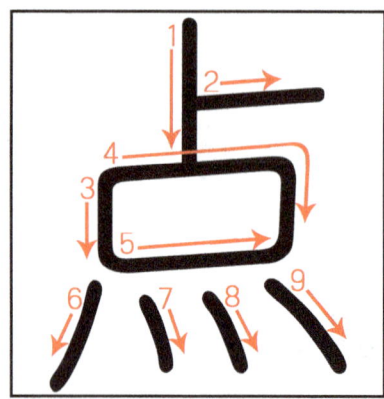

一点　Yīdiǎn　*a bit/a little*

点头　diǎntóu　*nod one's head*

有点　yǒudiǎn　*somewhat/a bit*

点心　diǎnxīn　*dim sum/pastry*

点钟　diǎnzhōng　*o'clock*

Strokes: 9

Radical: 灬 (火) huǒ
'fire'

Pinyin: diǎn

*Practice writing this character using the stroke order shown above.
When you're finished, circle the one that you like the best.*

点	点	点	点	点	点

點 点 点 点 点 点 点 点 点

My Character Picture for
DŌU all/both　DŪ capital

都

Describe your picture and write how you will remember what the character means and what it sounds like:

DŌU / DŪ

都
Simplified

都
Traditional

all, both / capital

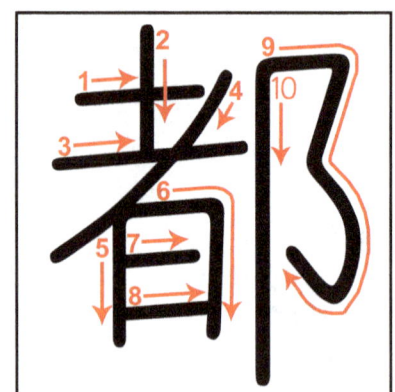

都 DŌU   *all, both*

首都 shǒuDŪ   *capital (of a country)*

不都 BùDŌU   *not all (of)*

大都 DàDŌU   *for the most part*

都市 DŪShì   *city*

Strokes: 10

Radical: 阝(邑) Yì 'region'

Pinyin: dōu / dū

Practice writing this character using the stroke order shown above.
When you're finished, circle the one that you like the best.

都 都 都 都 都 都

都 都 都 都 都 都 都

My Character Picture for
DUŌ *many/much*

Describe your picture and write how you will remember what the character means and what it sounds like:

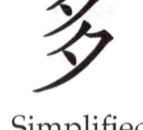

名字＿＿＿＿＿＿＿＿＿＿＿＿＿ ＿＿＿＿年 ＿＿＿月 ＿＿＿日

多 DUŌ 多

Simplified — many / much — Traditional

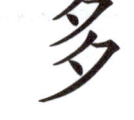

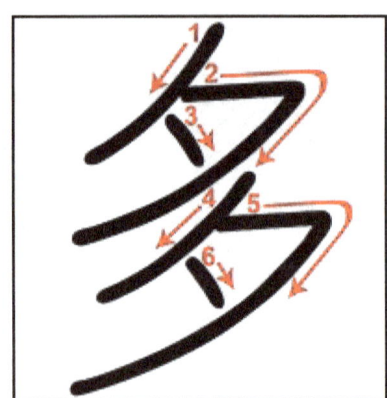

多 DUŌ *many*

多少 DUŌshǎo *how many/much*

多么 DUŌme* *so*

差不多 Chàbu*DUŌ *almost*

Strokes: 6

Radical: 夕 XĪ *'sunset'*

Pinyin: duō

Practice writing this character using the stroke order shown above.
When you're finished, circle the one that you like the best.

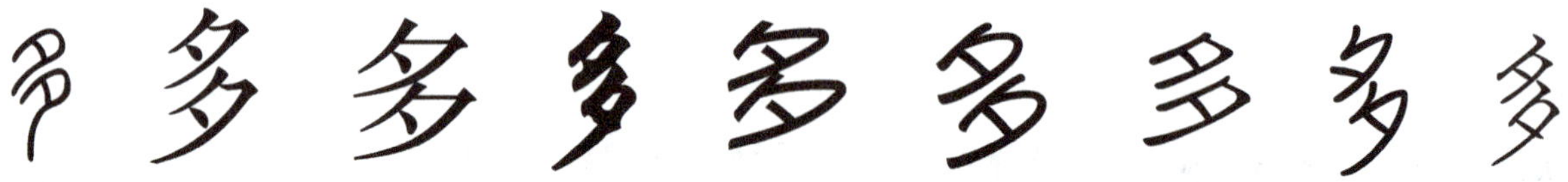

My Character Picture for
FĀ / fǎ / fa* *hair*

Describe your picture and write how you will remember what the character means and what it sounds like:

发
Simplified

FĀ / fǎ / fa*
hair

髮
Traditional

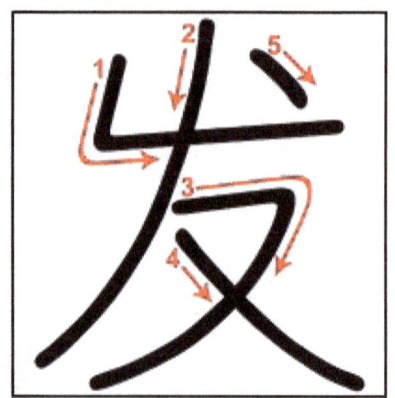

头发 tóUfa* *hair*

沙发 SHĀFĀ *sofa*

发生 fǎSHĒNG *happen, occur*

Strokes: 5

Radical: 又 Yòu
    'again'

Pinyin: fā

Practice writing this character using the stroke order shown above.
When you're finished, circle the one that you like the best.

发 发 发 发 发 发

发 发 发 发 发 发 发 发

My Character Picture for

fÚ   *clothes, serve*

服

Describe your picture and write how you will remember what the character means and what it sounds like:

服

Simplified

fÚ

clothes, serve

服

Traditional

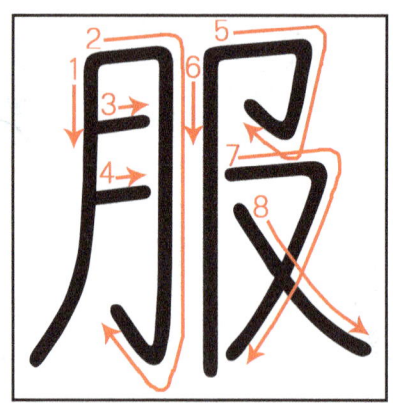

衣服 YĪfÚ *clothes*

服务员 fÚWùyuáN *waitress*

Strokes: 8

Radical: 月 Yuè '*moon*'

Pinyin: fú

Practice writing this character using the stroke order shown above.
When you're finished, circle the one that you like the best.

服　服　服　服　服　服

服 服 服 服 服 服 服 服

My Character Picture for
GĀO   *tall*

Describe your picture and write how you will remember what the character means and what it sounds like:

名字 --

名字_____ _____年 ____月 ____日

高

高 **Simplified**

GĀO
tall

高 **Traditional**

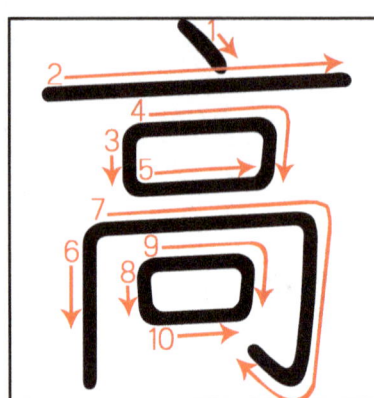

高 GĀO *tall*

高兴 GĀOXìng *happy*

最高 ZuìGĀO *highest*

高中 GĀOZHŌNG *high school*

高考 GĀOkǎo *college entrance exam*

Strokes: 10
Radical: 高 GĀO 'tall'
Pinyin: gāo

Practice writing this character using the stroke order shown above.
When you're finished, circle the one that you like the best.

My Character Picture for
Gè / ge*   (a measure word)

Describe your picture and write how you will remember what the character means and what it sounds like:

个
Simplified

Gè / ge*
(a measure word)

個
Traditional

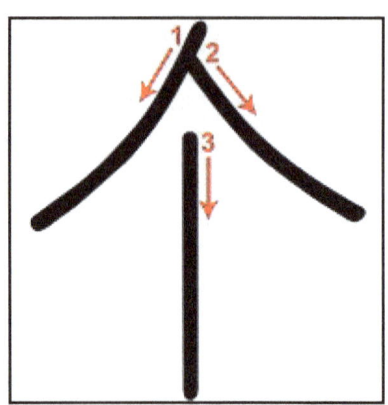

这个 Zhèige* this one

那个 / 哪个 Nàge* / něige* that one

个人 GèréN individual person

个子 Gèzi* body

个别 GèbiÉ individually

Strokes: 3

Radical: 丨 gǔn 'vertical stroke'

Pinyin: gè

Practice writing this character using the stroke order shown above.
When you're finished, circle the one that you like the best.

个 个 个 个 个 个

個 个 个 个 个 个 个 个 个

My Character Picture for
GĒN   with/and/to

跟

Describe your picture and write how you will remember what the character means and what it sounds like:

跟
Simplified

GĒN
with / and / to

跟
Traditional

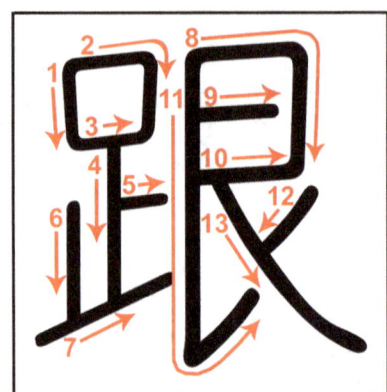

跟　GĒN　*with/and/to*

跟着　GĒNzhe*　*follow in the wake of*

脚跟　jiǎoGĒN　*heel*

翻跟头　FĀN GĒNtou*
　　　　turn a somersault

鞋跟　xiÉGĒN　*heel (of a shoe)*

Strokes: 13
Radical:  zÚ *'foot'*
Pinyin: gēn

Practice writing this character using the stroke order shown above.
When you're finished, circle the one that you like the best.

跟

My Character Picture for
guó   *country/state/nation*

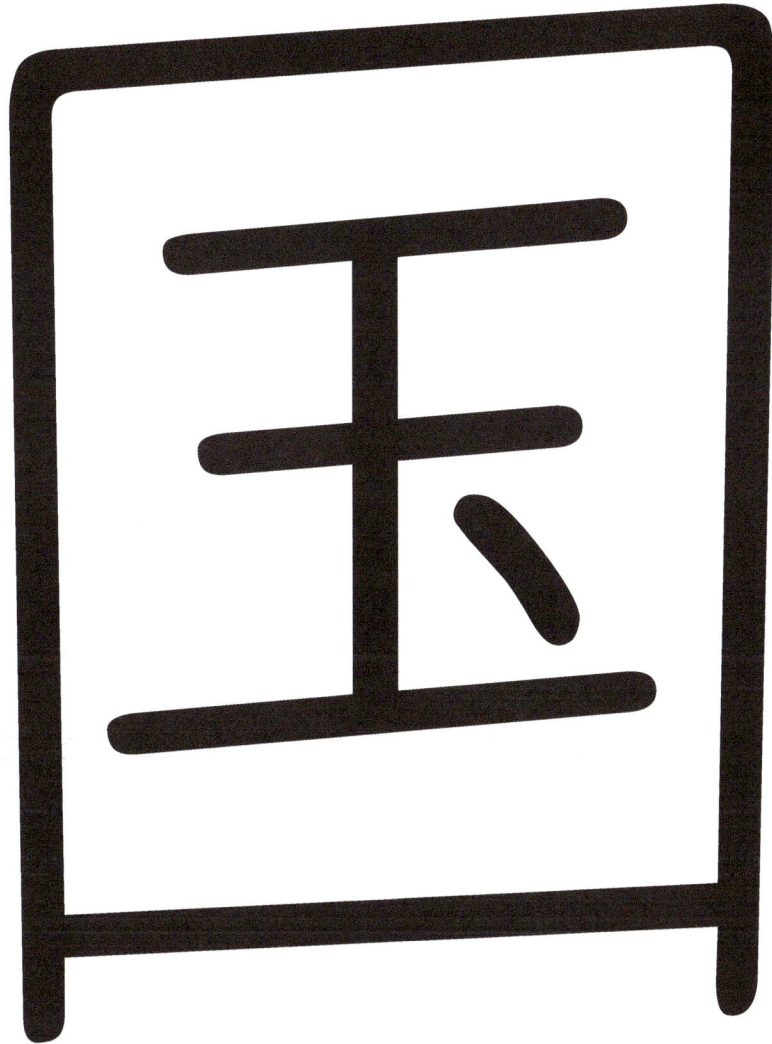

Describe your picture and write how you will remember what the character means and what it sounds like:

国

Simplified

guó

country / state / nation

國

Traditional

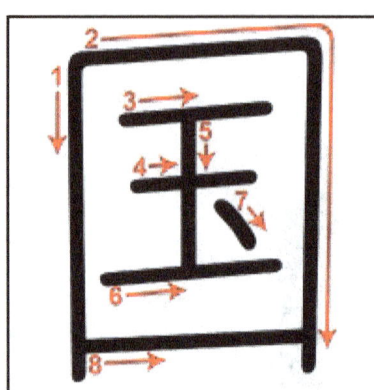

国家 guóJIĀ *nation*

祖国 zǔguó *Motherland*

国内 guóNèi *domestic*

国际 guóJì *international*

外国 Wàiguó *foreign country*

Strokes: 8

Radical: 口 wéI
'enclosure'

Pinyin: guó

Practice writing this character using the stroke order shown above.
When you're finished, circle the one that you like the best.

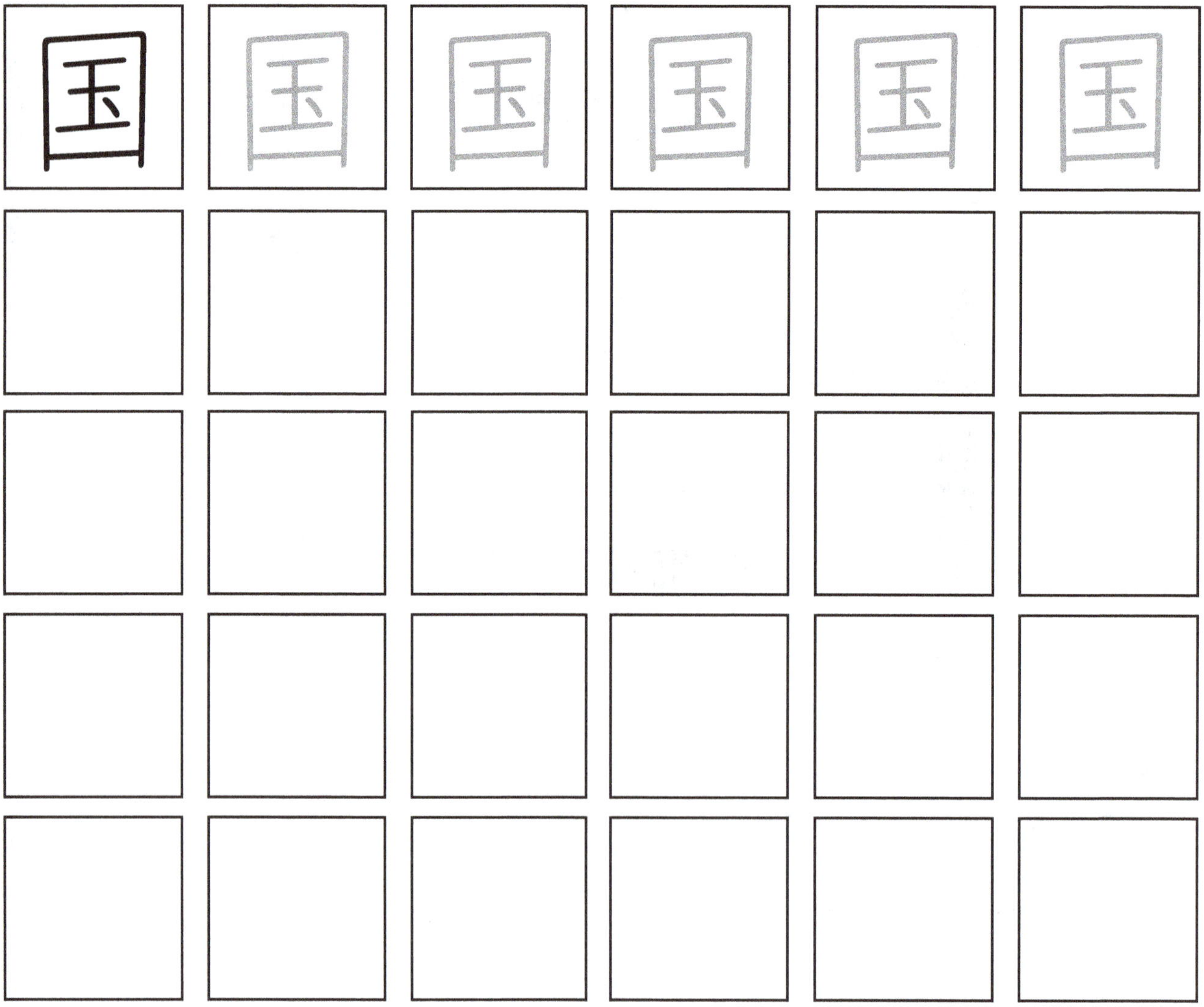

My Character Picture for
guǒ *fruit / if really*

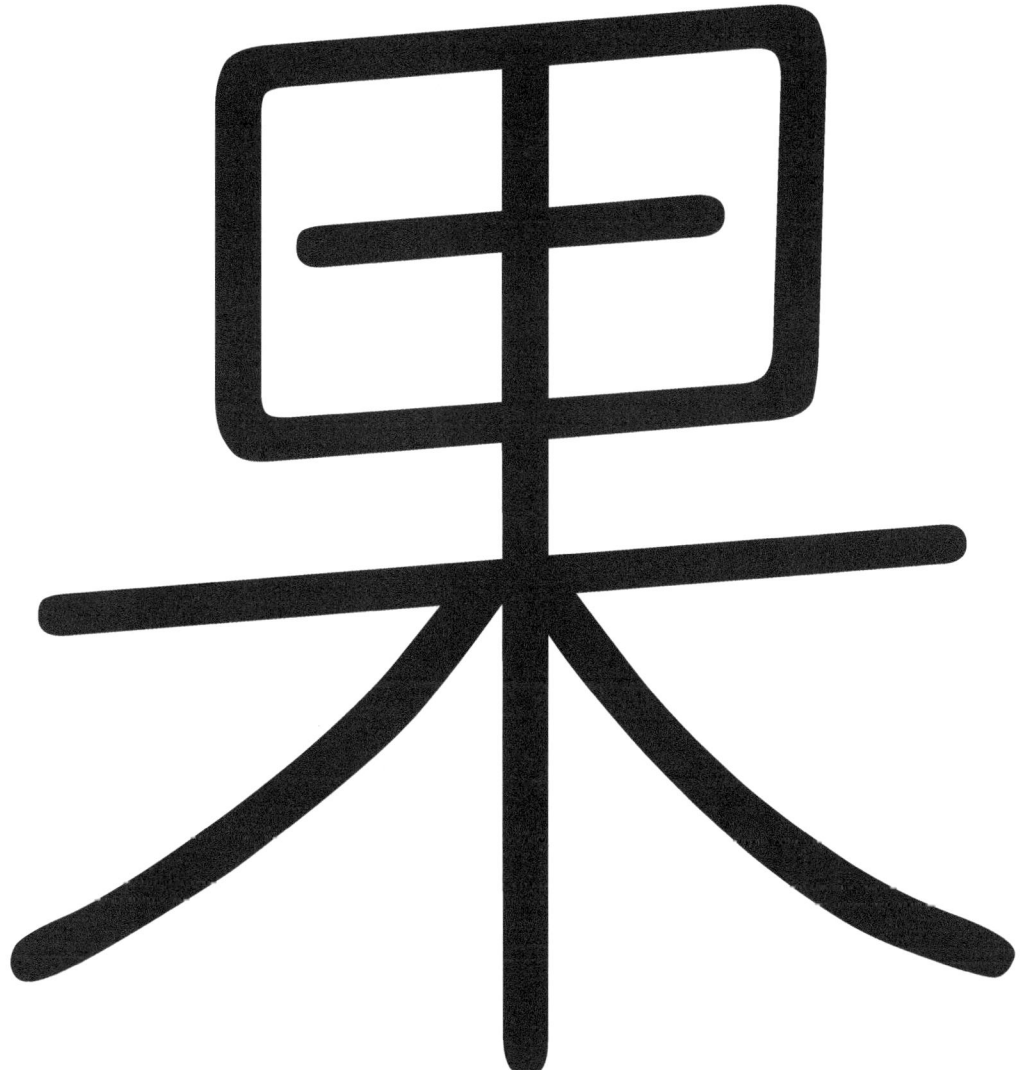

Describe your picture and write how you will remember what the character means and what it sounds like:

果
Simplified

guǒ
fruit / if really

果
Traditional

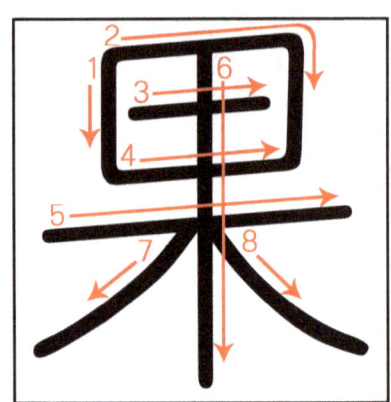

如果 rÚguǒ *if*

水果 shuǐguǒ *fruit*

苹果 pínGguǒ *apple*

果然 guǒráN *really; as expected*

结果 jiÉguǒ *finally; as the result*

Strokes: 8

Radical: 木 Mù *'tree'*

Pinyin: guǒ

Practice writing this character using the stroke order shown above.
When you're finished, circle the one that you like the best.

My Character Picture for

Hàn *Chinese (language)/Han nationality/Han Dynasty*

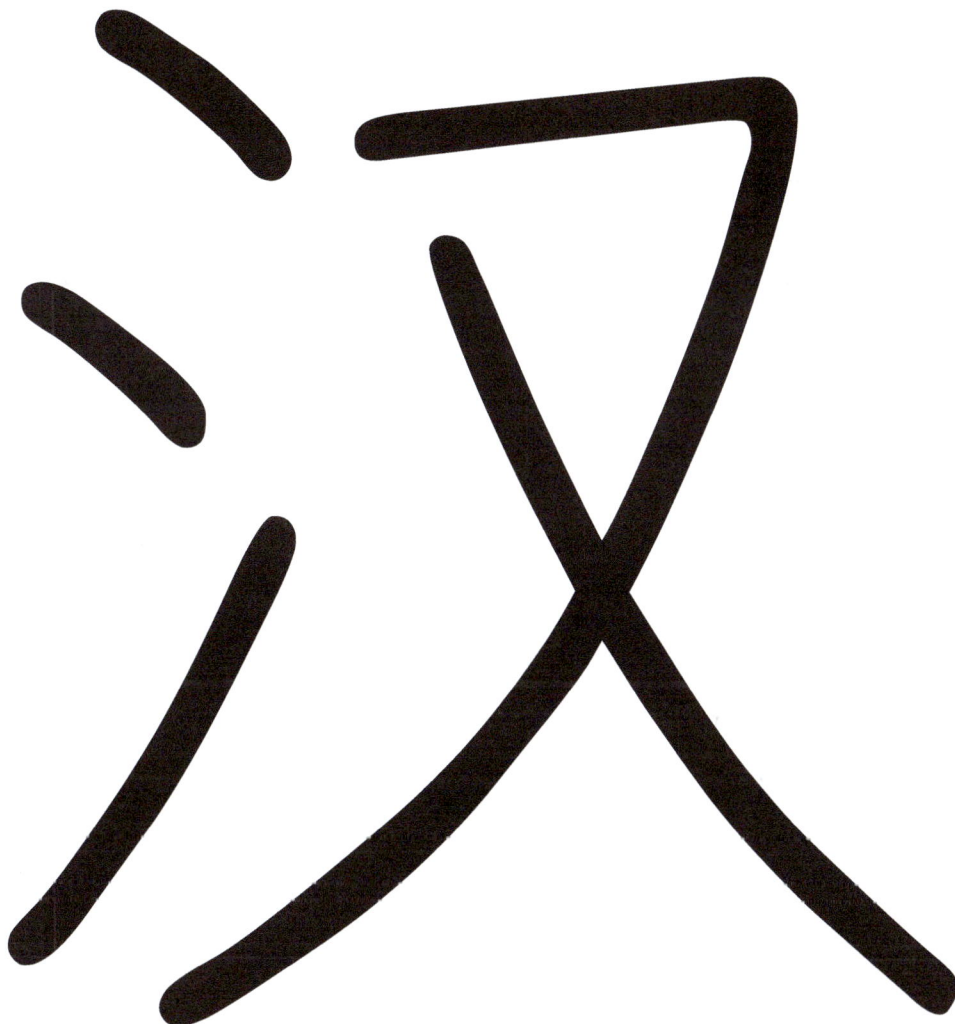

Describe your picture and write how you will remember what the character means and what it sounds like:

Hàn

Chinese (language) /
Han nationality / Han Dynasty

汉 Simplified

漢 Traditional

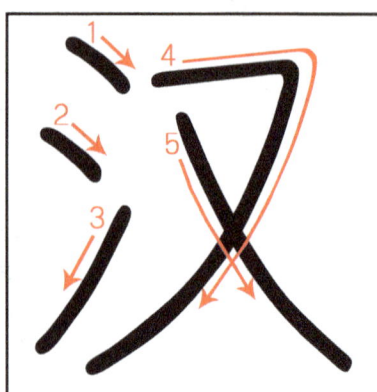

汉语　Hànyǔ　*Chinese (language)*

汉字　HànZì　*Chinese character*

汉堡包　HànbǎoBĀO　*hamburger*

武汉　wǔHàn　*Wuhan*
(capital of Hubei province)

好汉　hǎoHàn　*brave man; true hero*

Strokes: 5

Radical: 氵(水) shuǐ
'water'

Pinyin: hàn

Practice writing this character using the stroke order shown above.
When you're finished, circle the one that you like the best.

My Character Picture for
hǎo   *good*

Describe your picture and write how you will remember what the character means and what it sounds like:

好
Simplified

hǎo
good

好
Traditional

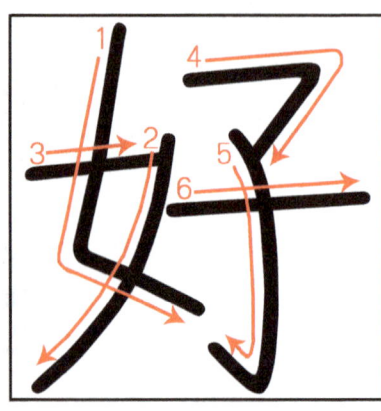

好 hǎo *good*

不好 Bùhǎo *bad*

好吃 hǎoCHĪ *good to eat, yummy*

好看 hǎoKàn *good-looking*

好像 hǎoXiàng *seem, be like*

Strokes: 6

Radical: 女 nǚ *'woman'*

Pinyin: hǎo

Practice writing this character using the stroke order shown above.
When you're finished, circle the one that you like the best.

My Character Picture for
HĒ   drink

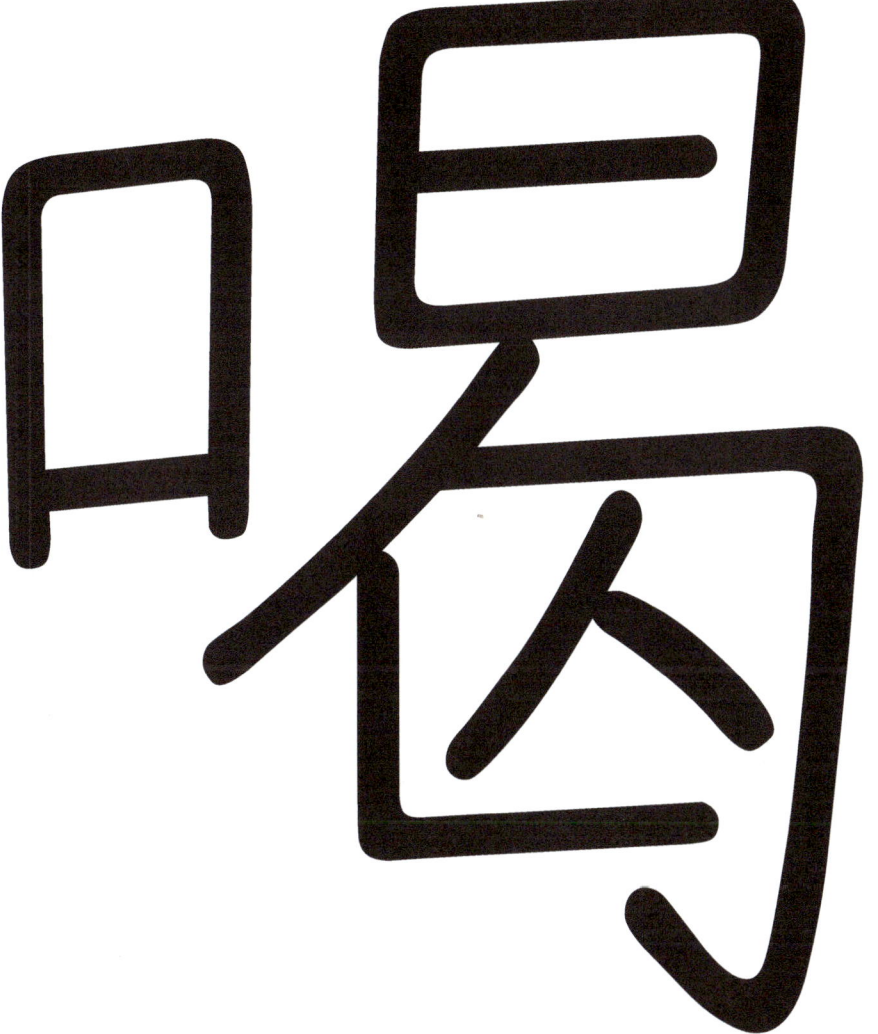

Describe your picture and write how you will remember what the character means and what it sounds like:

喝
Simplified

HĒ
drink

喝
Traditional

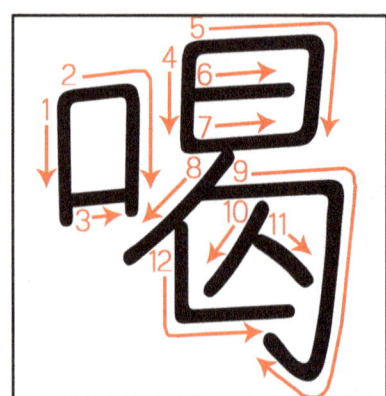

喝　HĒ　*drink*

喝水　HĒ shuǐ　*drink water*

好喝　hǎoHĒ　*good to drink, tasty*

喝茶　HĒ chÁ　*drink tea*

Strokes: 12

Radical: 口 kǒu
　　　　'mouth'

Pinyin: hē /hè

Practice writing this character using the stroke order shown above.
When you're finished, circle the one that you like the best.

喝 喝 喝 喝 喝 喝

喝 喝 喝 喝 喝 喝 喝 喝

My Character Picture for
hÉ / huo   and/with/harmony*

Describe your picture and write how you will remember what the character means and what it sounds like:

和
Simplified

hÉ/huo*
and/with/harmony

和
Traditional

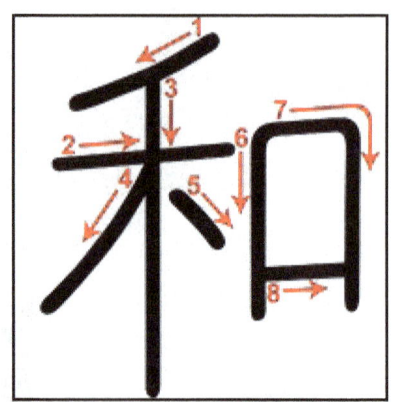

和 hÉ *and*
和平 hÉpínG *peace*
暖和 nuǎnhuo* *warm*
你和我 nǐ hÉ wǒ *you and I*

Strokes: 8
Radical: 口 kǒu
   '*mouth*'
Pinyin: hé

Practice writing this character using the stroke order shown above.
When you're finished, circle the one that you like the best.

My Character Picture for
hěn   very

Describe your picture and write how you will remember what the character means and what it sounds like:

很

Simplified

hěn

very

很

Traditional

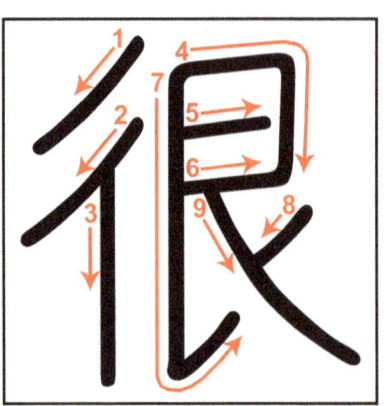

很　hěn　*very*

很好　hěnhǎo　*very good*

很不错　hěnbúcuò　*pretty good*

很想　hěnxiǎng　*anxious/eager to…*

Strokes: 9

Radical: 彳 Chì
　　　'a step with the left foot'

Pinyin: hěn

Practice writing this character using the stroke order shown above.
When you're finished, circle the one that you like the best.

很　很　很　很　很　很

很 很 很 很 很 很 很 很

My Character Picture for
Hòu   *rear/later*

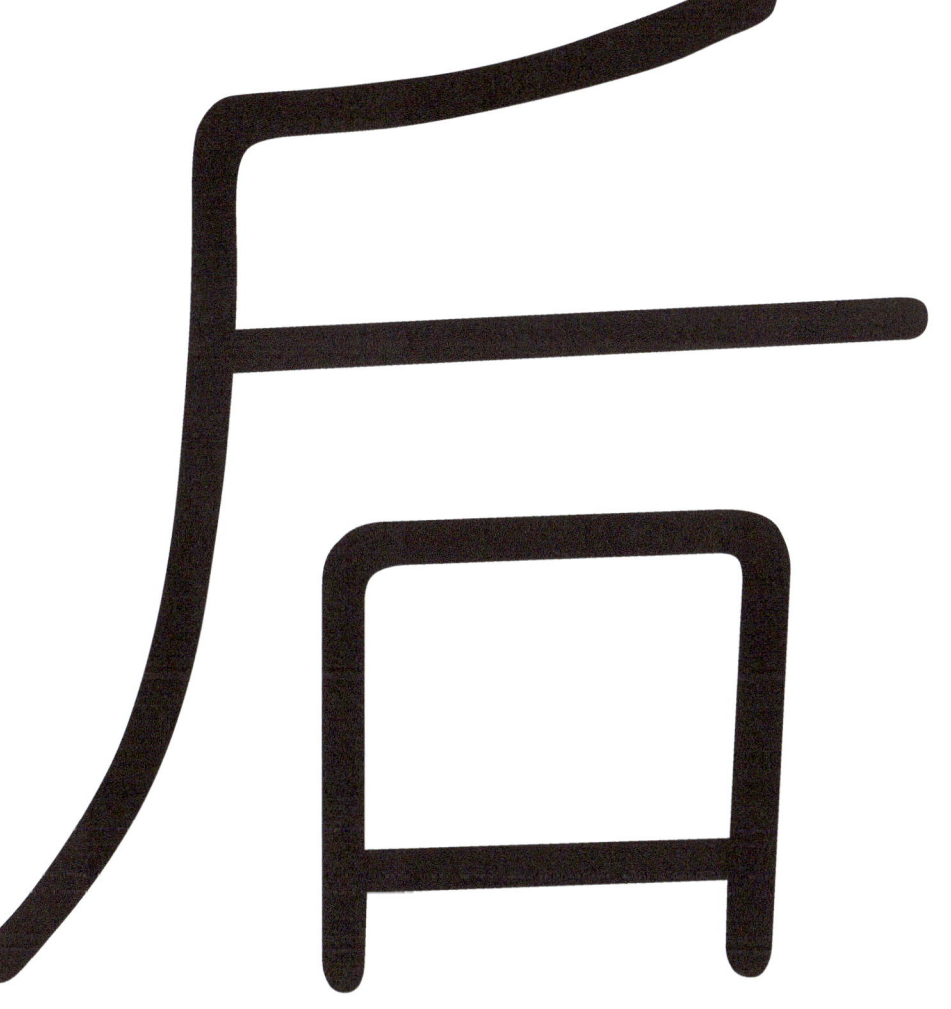

Describe your picture and write how you will remember what the character means and what it sounds like:

名字__________________ ______年 ____月 ____日

后 Hòu 后

Simplified — rear / later — Traditional

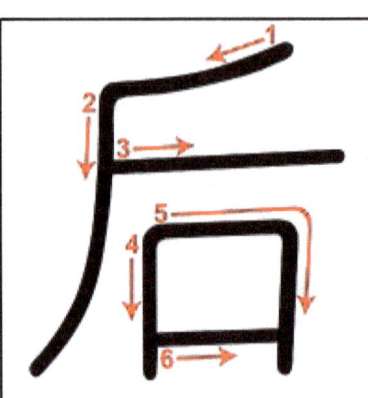

以后 yǐHòu *afterward*

最后 ZuìHòu *last; final*

后来 HòuláI *afterward; later*

然后 ráNHòu *and then; after that*

后面 Hòumian* *at the back; behind*

Strokes: 6

Radical: 口 kǒu *'mouth'*

Pinyin: hòu

Practice writing this character using the stroke order shown above.
When you're finished, circle the one that you like the best.

后	后	后	后	后	后

后 后 后 后 后 后 后 后 后

My Character Picture for

Hòu *time/wait*

Describe your picture and write how you will remember what the character means and what it sounds like:

候
Simplified

Hòu
time / wait

候
Traditional

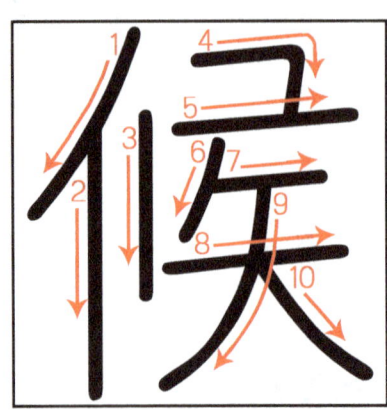

时候 shíhou* *(duration of; point in)*
time

气候 QìHòu *climate; situation*

有时候 yǒushíhou*(r) *sometimes;*
now and then

等候 děngHòu *wait; expect*

Strokes: 10
Radical: 亻（人）réN
　　　　　'*person*'
Pinyin: hòu

Practice writing this character using the stroke order shown above.
When you're finished, circle the one that you like the best.

候

名字________________________________ ________年 _____月 _____日

My Character Picture for

HUĀN *happy/joyous*

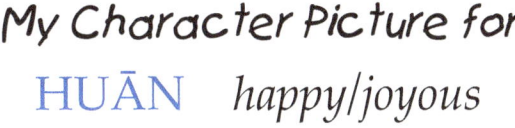

欢

Describe your picture and write how you will remember what the character means and what it sounds like:

欢
Simplified

HUĀN
happy / joyous

歡
Traditional

喜欢 xǐHUĀN *like*

欢迎 HUĀNyínG *welcome*

欢乐 HUĀNLè *happy, joyous*

欢笑 HUĀNXiào *laugh heartily*

Strokes: 6

Radical: 欠 Qiàn 'owe'

Pinyin: huān

Practice writing this character using the stroke order shown above.
When you're finished, circle the one that you like the best.

My Character Picture for
jǐ   *how many/a few*

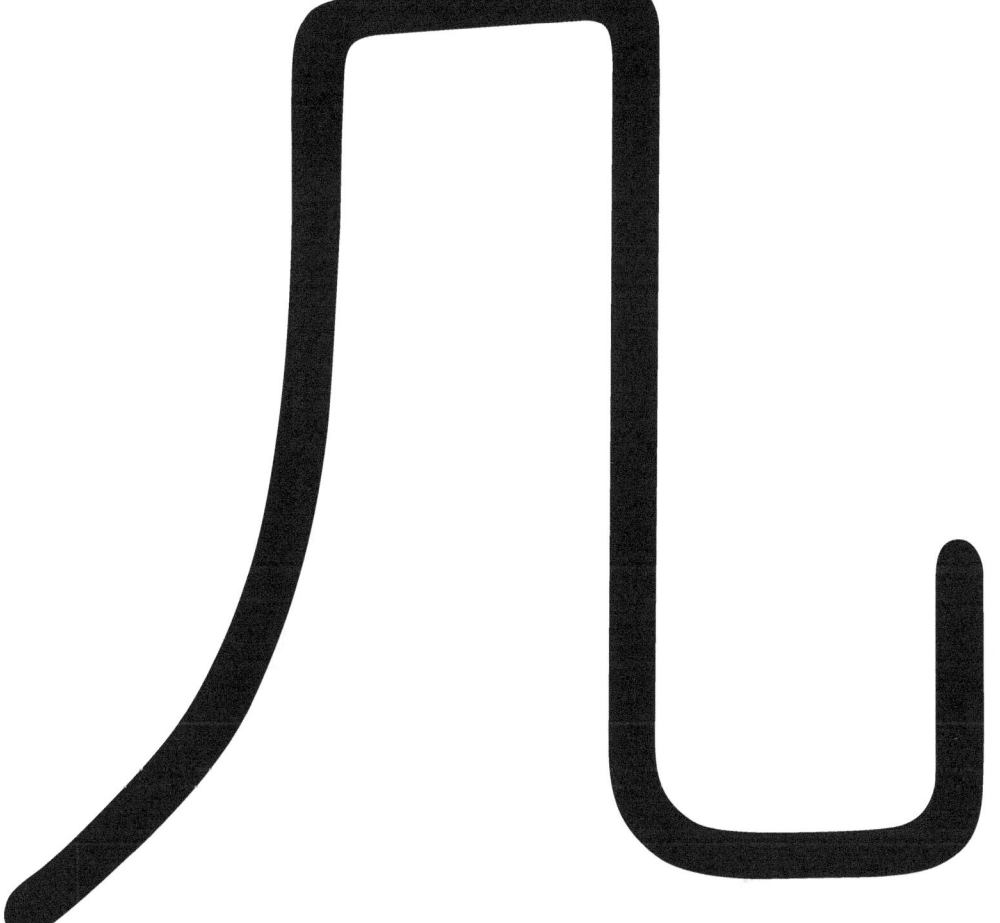

Describe your picture and write how you will remember what the character means and what it sounds like:

几

Simplified

jǐ

how many / a few

幾

Traditional

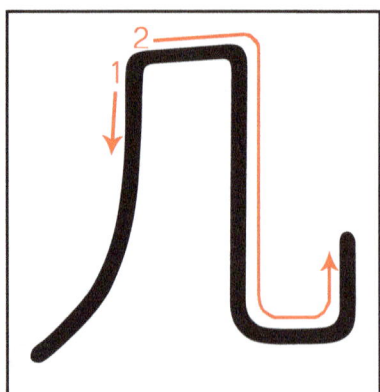

几 jǐ   *how many/a few*

几个   jǐge*   *a few; several; how many?*

好几个   hǎoji*ge*   *several*

第几   Dì-jǐ   *which one (in sequence)*

Strokes: 2

Radical: 几 jǐ *'some'*

Pinyin: jǐ

*Practice writing this character using the stroke order shown above.
When you're finished, circle the one that you like the best.*

My Character Picture for
JIĀ *family/home*

Describe your picture and write how you will remember what the character means and what it sounds like:

家
Simplified

JIĀ
family / home

家
Traditional

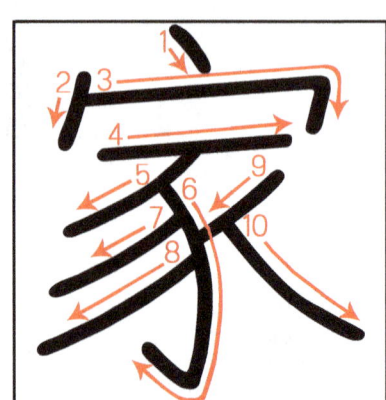

家庭　JIĀtínG　*family; household*

国家　guÓJIĀ　*country; nation*

回家　huÍJIĀ　*return home*

大家　DàJIĀ　*everyone*

作家　ZuòJIĀ　*writer; author*

Strokes: 10

Radical: 宀 miáN *'roof'*

Pinyin: jiā

Practice writing this character using the stroke order shown above.
When you're finished, circle the one that you like the best.

家　家　家　家　家　家

家 家 家 家 家 家 家 家

名字____________________ ________年 ______月 ______日

My Character Picture for

JĪN *today*

今

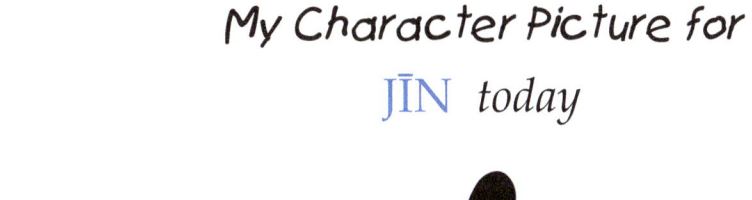

Describe your picture and write how you will remember what the character means and what it sounds like:

Simplified

JĪN

today, now

Traditional

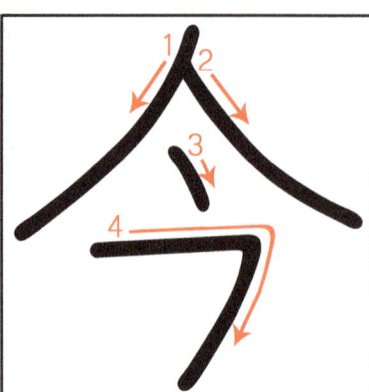

今天　JĪNTIĀN　*today*

今年　JĪNniáN　*this year*

今日　JĪNRì　*today*

今后　JĪNHòu　*from now on*

至今　ZhìJĪN　*until now*

Strokes: 4

Radical: 人 réN
　　　　　'person'

Pinyin: jīn

Practice writing this character using the stroke order shown above.
When you're finished, circle the one that you like the best.

54

My Character Picture for
Jìu *just/simply/right away*

就

Describe your picture and write how you will remember what the character means and what it sounds like:

就
Simplified

Jìu
just / simply / right away

就
Traditional

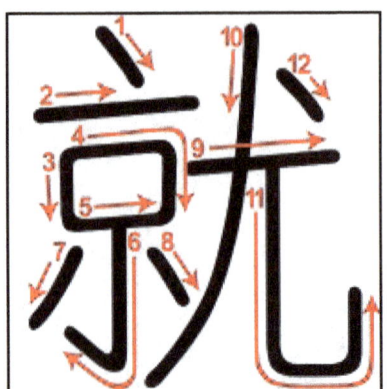

就 Jìu *even if, right away*

就是 JìuShì *that is*

就是了 JìuShìle* *that's it precisely*

Strokes: 12

Radical: 尢 WĀNG
'lame'

Pinyin: jiù

Practice writing this character using the stroke order shown above.
When you're finished, circle the one that you like the best.

就 就 就 就 就 就

就 就 就 就 就 就 就 就

My Character Picture for

Kàn *see/look at/watch*

Describe your picture and write how you will remember what the character means and what it sounds like:

看
Simplified

Kàn
see / look at / watch

看
Traditional

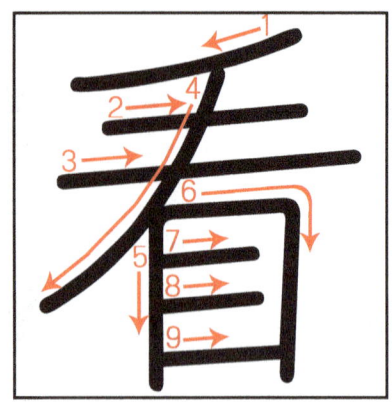

看　Kàn　*see, look at, watch*

看到　KànDào　*catch sight of, see*

看见　KànJiàn　*catch sight of, see*

看看　Kànkan*　*take a look at*

好看　hǎoKàn　*good-looking*

Strokes: 9

Radical: 目 Mù 'eye'

Pinyin: kàn

Practice writing this character using the stroke order shown above.
When you're finished, circle the one that you like the best.

看　看　看　看　看　看

看 看 看 看 看 看 看 看

My Character Picture for
kě   *can/may/able to/(particle used for emphasis)*

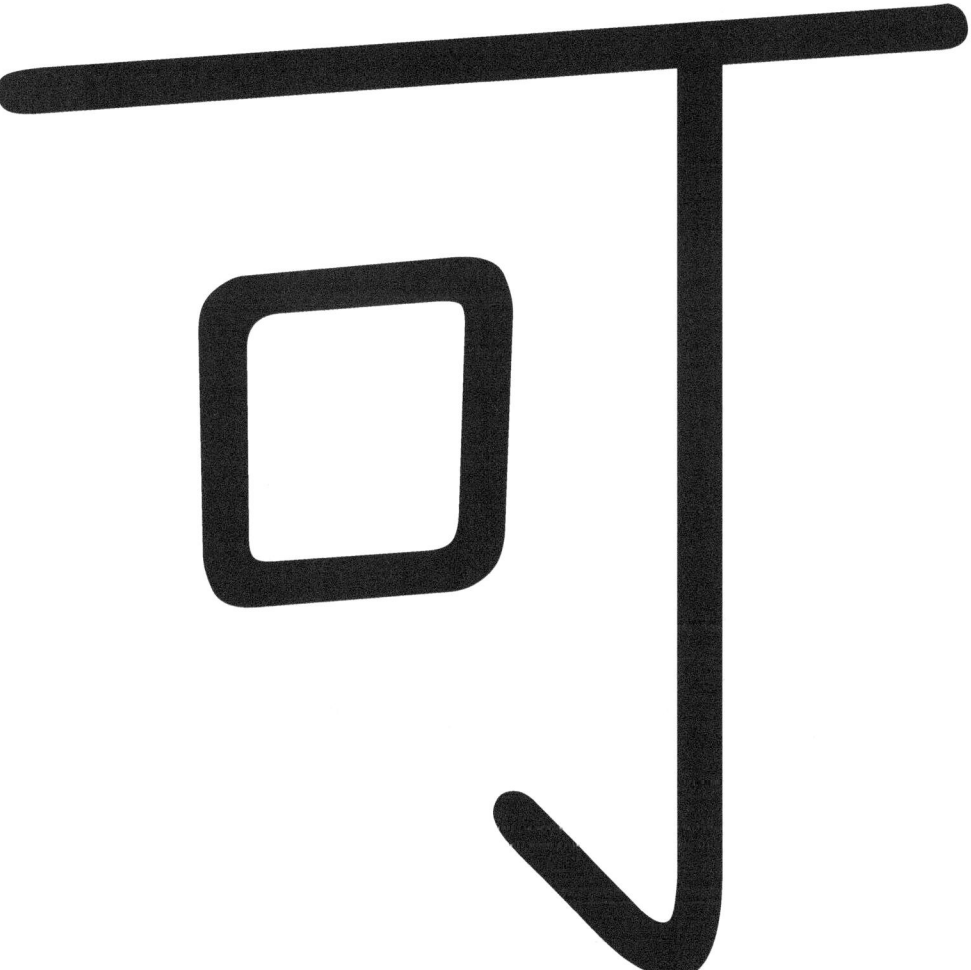

Describe your picture and write how you will remember what the character means and what it sounds like:

Simplified

kě

can / may / able to /
(particle used for emphasis)

Traditional

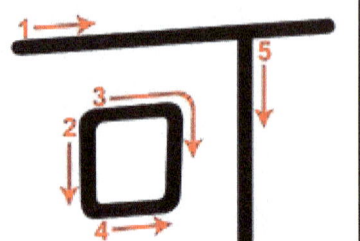

可以 kěyǐ *allowed to*

可是 kěShì *but*

可能 kěnénG *possibly*

可怜 kěliáN *pitiable*

可爱 kě'Ài *cute*

Strokes: 5

Radical: 口 kǒu
'mouth'

Pinyin: kě

Practice writing this character using the stroke order shown above.
When you're finished, circle the one that you like the best.

My Character Picture for

KŪ *cry/weep*

Describe your picture and write how you will remember what the character means and what it sounds like:

哭
Simplified

KŪ
cry / weep

哭
Traditional

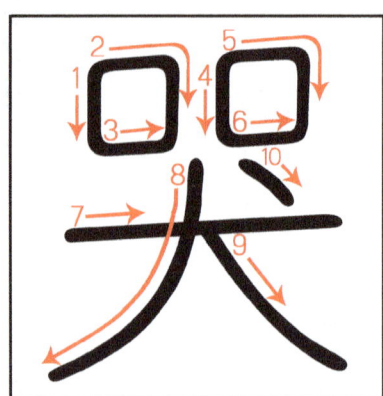

哭　KŪ　*cry*

大哭　DàKŪ　*cry loudly*

痛哭　TòngKŪ　*weep bitterly*

哭恼　KŪNào　*throw a tantrum*

号哭　háOKŪ　*wail*

Strokes: 10

Radical: 口 kǒu
　　　　'mouth'

Pinyin: kū

Practice writing this character using the stroke order shown above.
When you're finished, circle the one that you like the best.

My Character Picture for
Kù   cool/extreme/cruel

Describe your picture and write how you will remember what the character means and what it sounds like:

酷

Kù

酷
Simplified

cool / extreme / cruel

Traditional

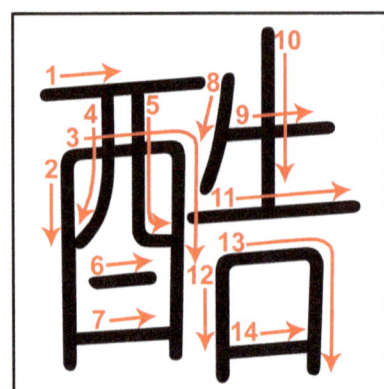

酷 Kù *cool*

残酷 cáNKù *cruel; brutal*

优酷 YŌUKù *"Youku"*
           (Chinese Youtube)

酷热 KùRè *extremely hot (weather)*

Strokes: 14

Radical: 酉 yǒu
         'wine'

Pinyin: kù

Practice writing this character using the stroke order shown above.
When you're finished, circle the one that you like the best.

My Character Picture for

láI   come/arrive

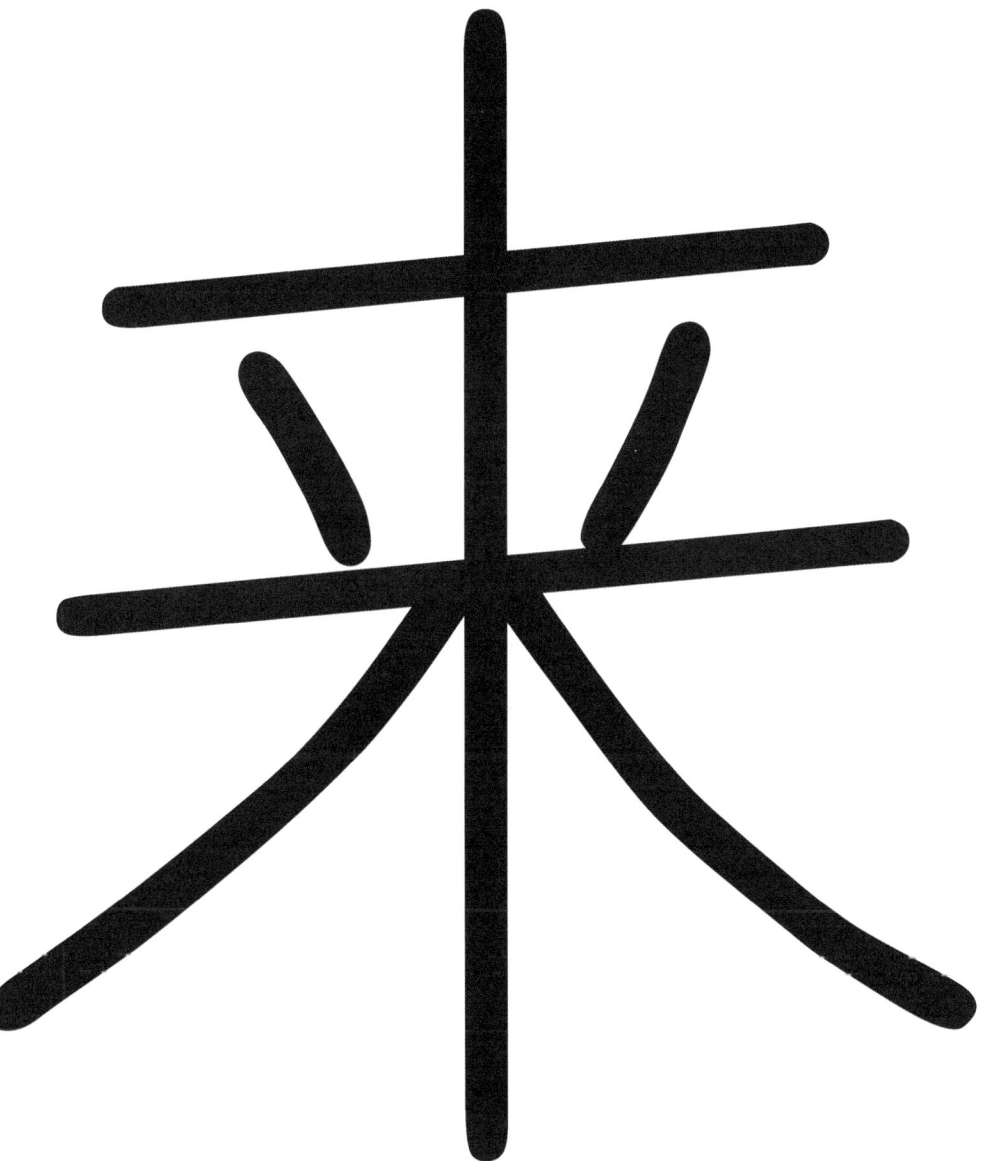

Describe your picture and write how you will remember what the character means and what it sounds like:

来
Simplified

láI
come / arrive

來
Traditional

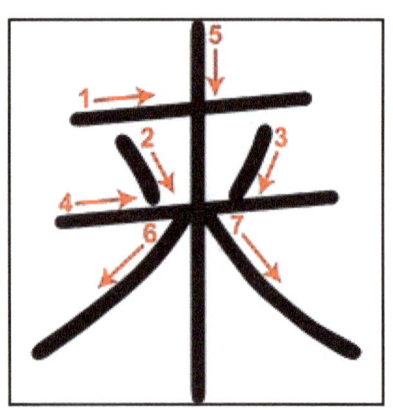

来 láI *come*

起来 qǐláI *get up*

出来 CHŪláI *come out*

下来 XiàláI *come down*

过来 GuòláI *come over*

Strokes: 7

Radical: 木 Mù 'tree'

Pinyin: lái

Practice writing this character using the stroke order shown above.
When you're finished, circle the one that you like the best.

来 来 来 来 来 来

My Character Picture for

le*/liǎo (completed action or change of state marker)

Describe your picture and write how you will remember what the character means and what it sounds like:

----

le* / liǎo

(completed action or change of state marker)

了 Simplified

了 Traditional

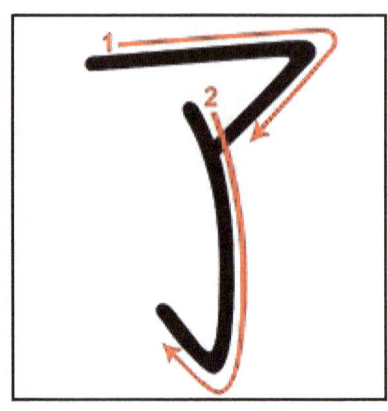

为 了　Wèile*　*in order to*

了 解　liǎojiÉ　*understand*

除 了　chÚle*　*except*

极 了　jÍle*　*extremely*

算 了　Suànle*　*that's the end of it!*

Strokes: 2

Radical: 亅 juÉ *'a barb'*

Pinyin: le / liǎo

Practice writing this character using the stroke order shown above.
When you're finished, circle the one that you like the best.

了

了 了 了 了 了 了 了 了

My Character Picture for
ma*/ mÁ (question tag)

Describe your picture and write how you will remember what the character means and what it sounds like:

吗

Simplified

ma* / mÁ

(question tag)

嗎

Traditional

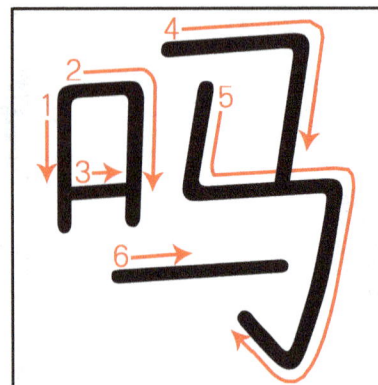

吗 ma* *(yes/no question)*

不是吗 bÚ Shì ma* *isn't that so?*

干吗 GànmÁ *Why? Whatever for? What's up?*

Strokes: 6

Radical: 口 kǒu 'mouth'

Pinyin: ma

Practice writing this character using the stroke order shown above.
When you're finished, circle the one that you like the best.

My Character Picture for
mǎi   *buy*

Describe your picture and write how you will remember what the character means and what it sounds like:

买　mǎi　買

Simplified　**buy**　**Traditional**

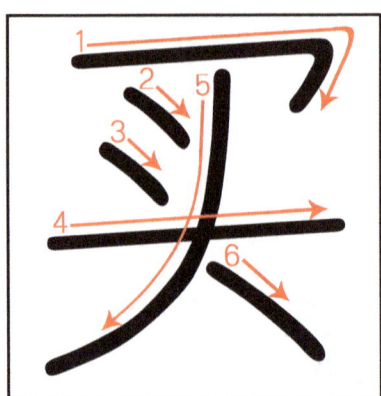

买　mǎi　*buy*

买卖　mǎimai*　*buy and sell*

买单　mǎiDĀN　*bill, tab*

买票　mǎiPiào　*buy tickets*

牙买加　yÁmǎiJIĀ　*Jamaica*

Strokes: 6

Radical: 一 (乙) Yǐ
'second'

Pinyin: mǎi

**Practice writing this character using the stroke order shown above.
When you're finished, circle the one that you like the best.**

My Character Picture for

Mài   *sell*

Describe your picture and write how you will remember what the character means and what it sounds like:

卖
Simplified

Mài
sell

賣
Traditional

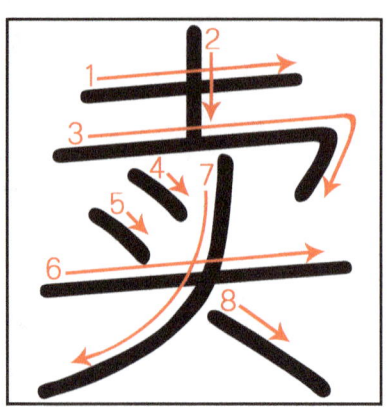

卖 Mài *sell*

买卖 mǎimai* *buy and sell*

卖给 Màigěi *sell to*

卖完 MàiwáN *sold out*

Strokes: 8

Radical: 十 shí *'ten'*

Pinyin: mài

Practice writing this character using the stroke order shown above.
When you're finished, circle the one that you like the best.

My Character Picture for

me*   *(interrogative particle)*

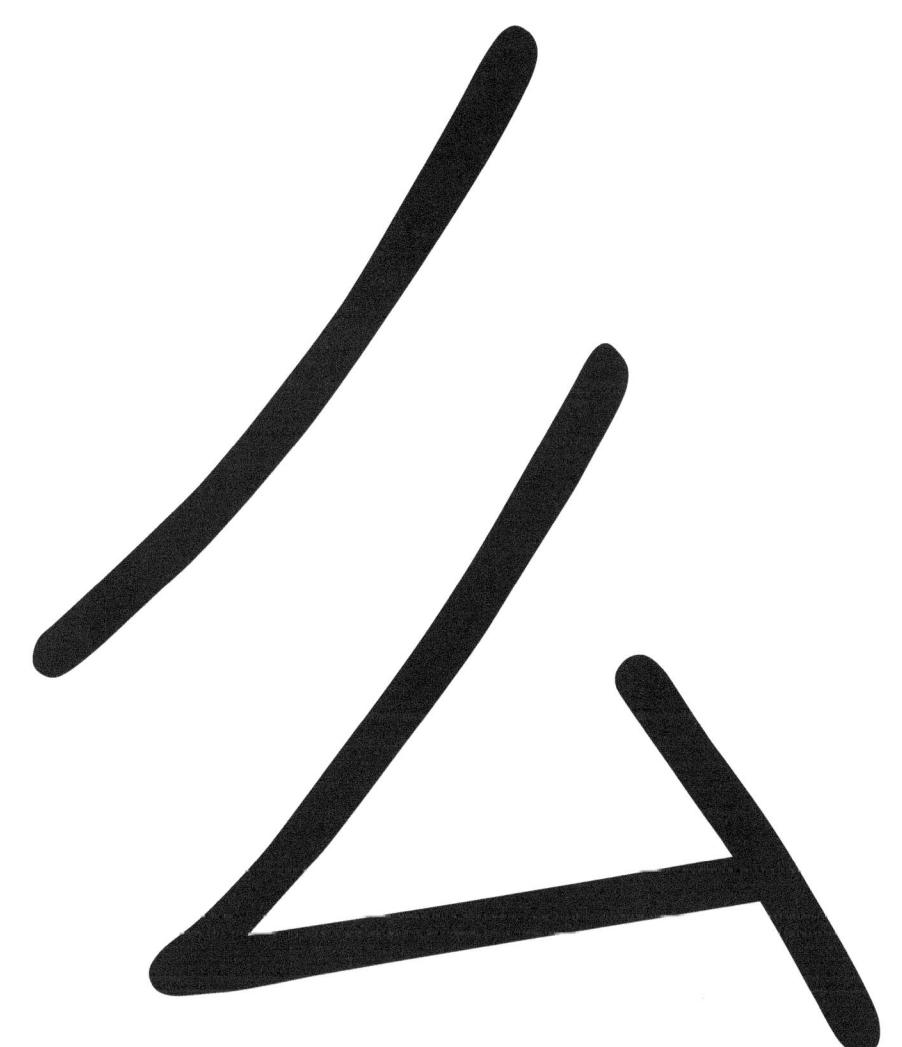

Describe your picture and write how you will remember what the character means and what it sounds like:

么

Simplified

me*

(interrogative particle)

麼

Traditional

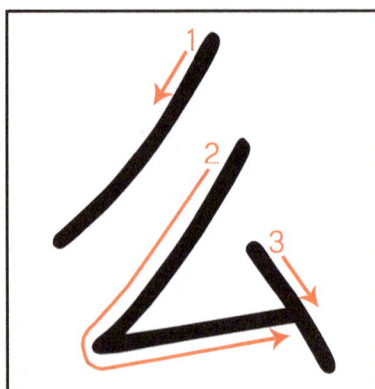

什么 shéNme* *what*

怎么 zěnme* *how*

为什么 WèishéNme* *why*

怎么样 zěnme* yang*
how are things?

没什么 méI shéNme* *never mind*

Strokes: 3

Radical: 丿 zhÚ
　　　　'stroke to the left'

Pinyin: me

Practice writing this character using the stroke order shown above.
When you're finished, circle the one that you like the best.

My Character Picture for
mÉI *not*

Describe your picture and write how you will remember what the character means and what it sounds like:

名字＿＿＿＿＿＿＿＿＿＿＿＿＿＿＿＿＿＿ ＿＿＿＿年 ＿＿＿月 ＿＿＿日

没

Simplified

mÉI

not

没

Traditional

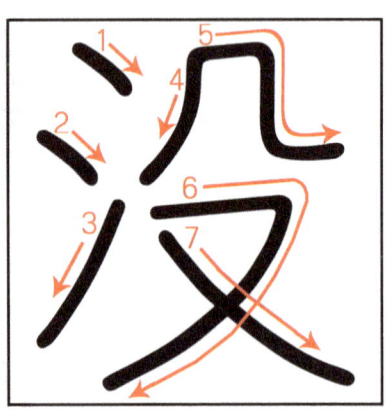

没有   mÉIyǒu   *not have; there is not*

没事   mÉIShì   *it's nothing;*
                         it doesn't matter

没用   mÉIYòng   *useless*

没意思   mÉIYìsi*   *boring*

没关系   mÉI GUĀNxi*   *it doesn't matter*

Strokes: 7

Radical: 氵(水) shuǐ
         'water'

Pinyin: méi

Practice writing this character using the stroke order shown above.
When you're finished, circle the one that you like the best.

没 没 没 没 没 没

没 没 没 没 没 没 没

My Character Picture for
měi   *beautiful, beauty*

Describe your picture and write how you will remember what the character means and what it sounds like:

美

Simplified

mĕi

beautiful, beauty

美

Traditional

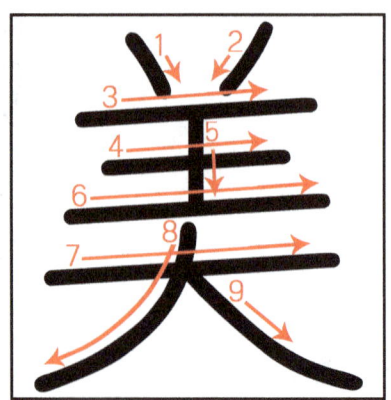

美国 mĕiguÓ *America*

美丽 mĕiLì *beautiful*

美元 mĕiyuáN *US dollar*

北美洲 bĕimĕiZHŌU
North America

南美洲 náNmĕiZHŌU
South America

Strokes: 9

Radical: 羊 yánG
'goat'

Pinyin: mĕi

**Practice writing this character using the stroke order shown above.
When you're finished, circle the one that you like the best.**

美

My Character Picture for
men* *(plural marker for pronouns and a few animate nouns)*

Describe your picture and write how you will remember what the character means and what it sounds like:

们
Simplified

men*
(plural marker for pronouns
and a few animate nouns)

們
Traditional

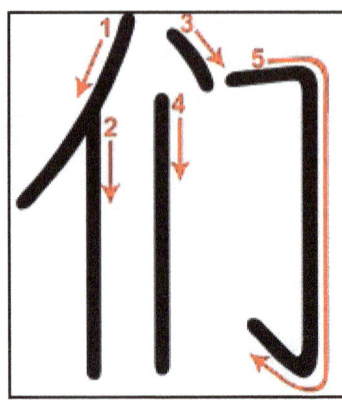

我们 wǒmen* *we*

他们／她们 TĀmen* *they*

你们 nǐmen* *you-all*

同学们 tónGxuÉmen* *students*

咱们 záNmen* *we (but not you)*

Strokes: 5

Radical: 亻(人) réN
'*person*'

Pinyin: men

*Practice writing this character using the stroke order shown above.
When you're finished, circle the one that you like the best.*

们	们	们	们	们	们

們 们 们 们 们 们 们 們

My Character Picture for
mínG   name

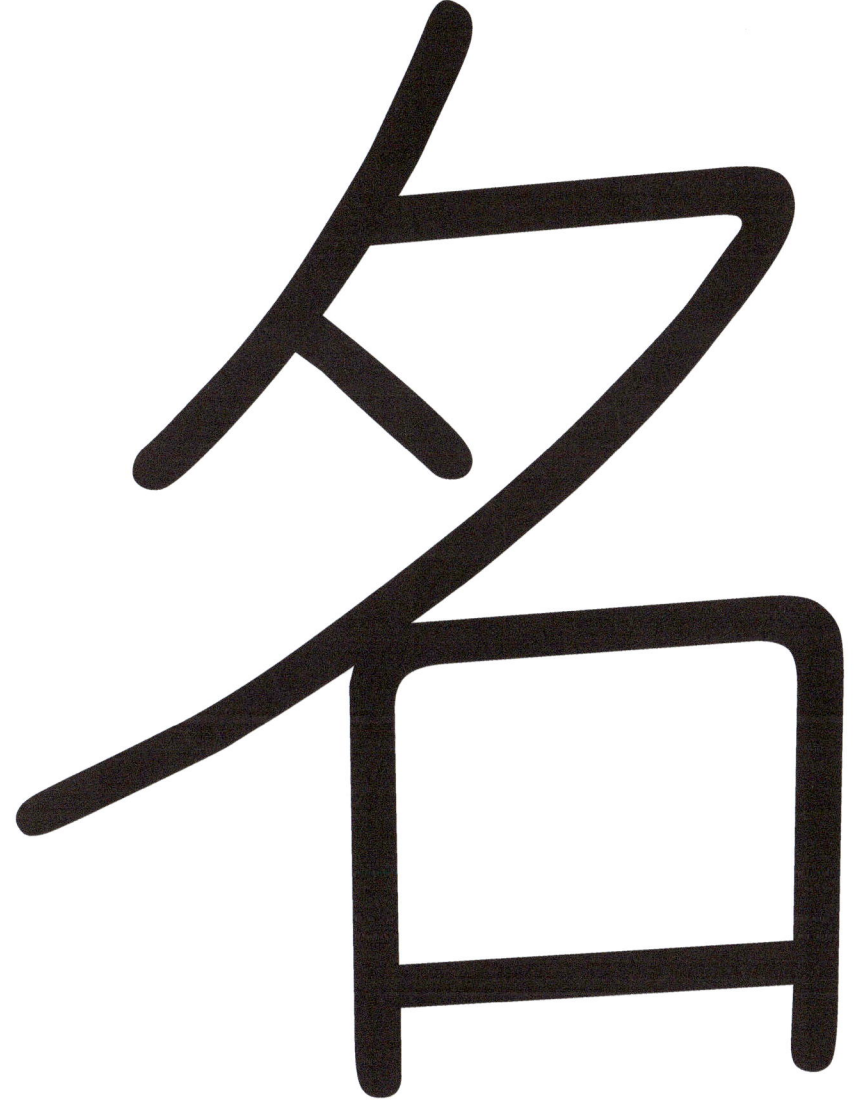

Describe your picture and write how you will remember what the character means and what it sounds like:

名字_____ _____年 _____月 _____日

名
Simplified

mínG

name

名
Traditional

名字　mínGzi*　(a person's) name

姓名　XìngmínG　full name

有名　yǒumínG　well-known, famous

名牌　mínGpáI brandname

名词　mínGcÍ　noun

Strokes: 6

Radical: 口 kǒu
'mouth'

Pinyin: míng

Practice writing this character using the stroke order shown above.
When you're finished, circle the one that you like the best.

名　名　名　名　名　名

名 名 名 名 名 名 名 名

84

My Character Picture for
mínG *bright/clear*

Describe your picture and write how you will remember what the character means and what it sounds like:

明
Simplified

mínG
bright/clear

明
Traditional

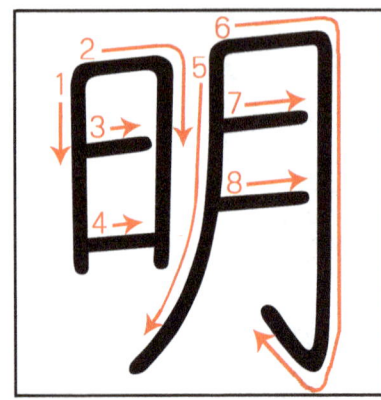

明白　mínGbai*　*understand/clear*

明天　mínGTIĀN　*tomorrow*

三明治　SĀNmínGZhì　*sandwich*

聪明　CŌNGming* *clever, intelligent*

明年　mínGniàN　*next year*

Strokes: 8

Radical: 日 Rì
'the sun'

Pinyin: míng

*Practice writing this character using the stroke order shown above.
When you're finished, circle the one that you like the best.*

明　明　明　明　明　明

明　明　明　明　明　明　明　明

My Character Picture for
nǎ *which / where / how*

哪

Describe your picture and write how you will remember what the character means and what it sounds like:

哪

nǎ

哪 Simplified

which / where / how

哪 Traditional

哪 nǎ *which*

哪里 / 哪儿 nǎlǐ / nǎr *where*

哪个 nǎge* *which*

哪些 nǎXIĒ *which ones*

哪边 nǎBIĀN *which side*

Strokes: 9

Radical: 口 kǒu 'mouth'

Pinyin: nǎ / nèi

Practice writing this character using the stroke order shown above. When you're finished, circle the one that you like the best.

哪	哪	哪	哪	哪	哪

哪 哪 哪 哪 哪 哪 哪 哪

My Character Picture for
Nà   *that / those*

Describe your picture and write how you will remember what the character means and what it sounds like:

那

Simplified

Nà

that / those

那

Traditional

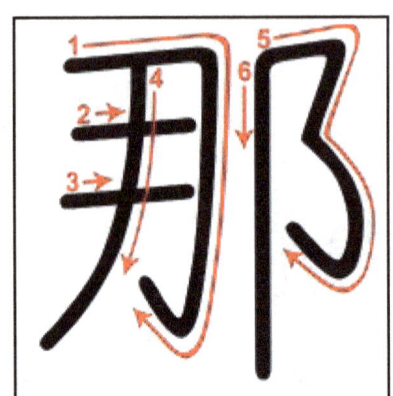

那么 Nàme* so

那样 NàYàng in that way

那些 NàXIĒ those

那里 / 那儿 Nàli* / Nàr there

那个 Nàge* that one

Strokes: 6

Radical: 阝(邑) Yì 'region'

Pinyin: nà

Practice writing this character using the stroke order shown above.
When you're finished, circle the one that you like the best.

My Character Picture for
náN   *man*

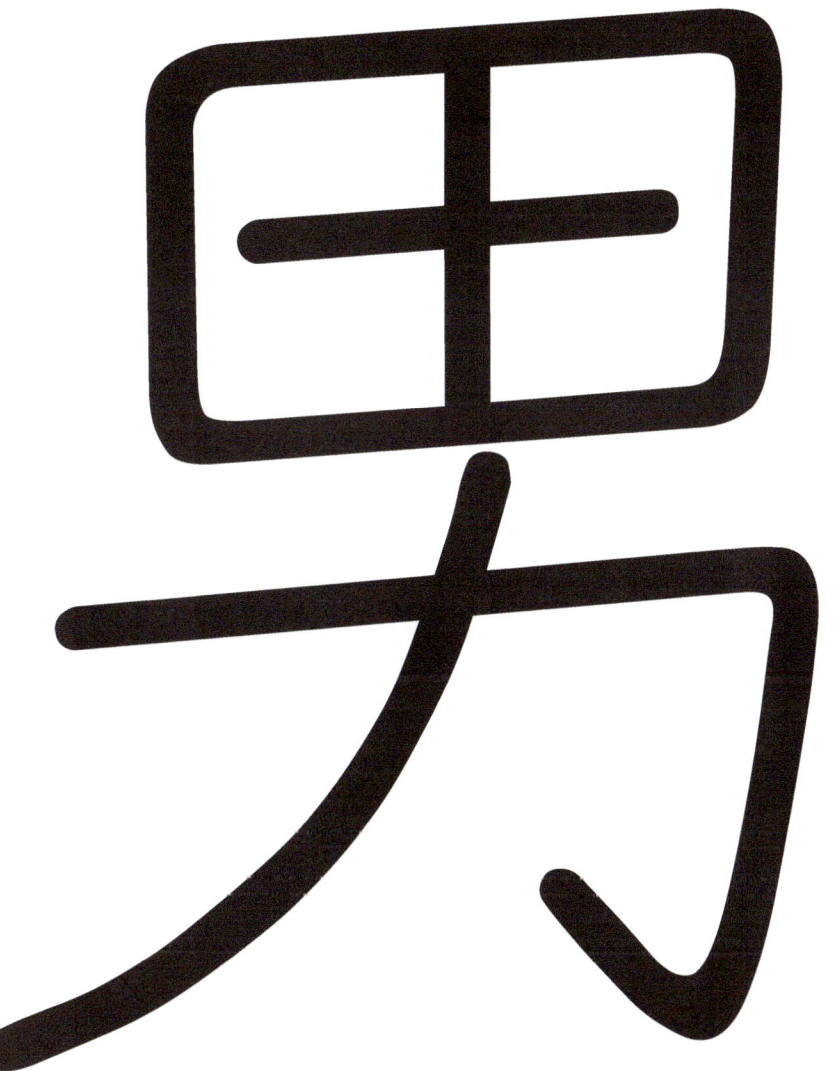

Describe your picture and write how you will remember what the character means and what it sounds like:

男
Simplified

man

男
Traditional

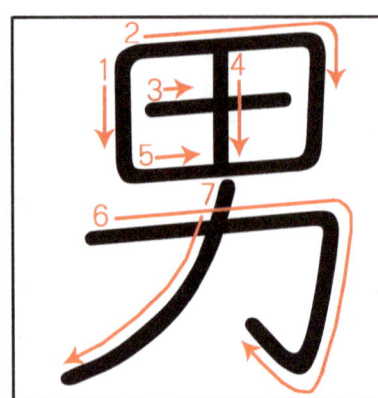

男人 náNréN *man*

男孩 náNháI *boy*

男厕所 náNCèsuǒ *men's toilet*

男女 náN-nǚ *men and women*

男生 náNSHĒNG *male student*

Strokes: 7

Radical: 田 tiáN *'field'*

Pinyin: nán

Practice writing this character using the stroke order shown above.
When you're finished, circle the one that you like the best.

My Character Picture for
nǐ   *you*

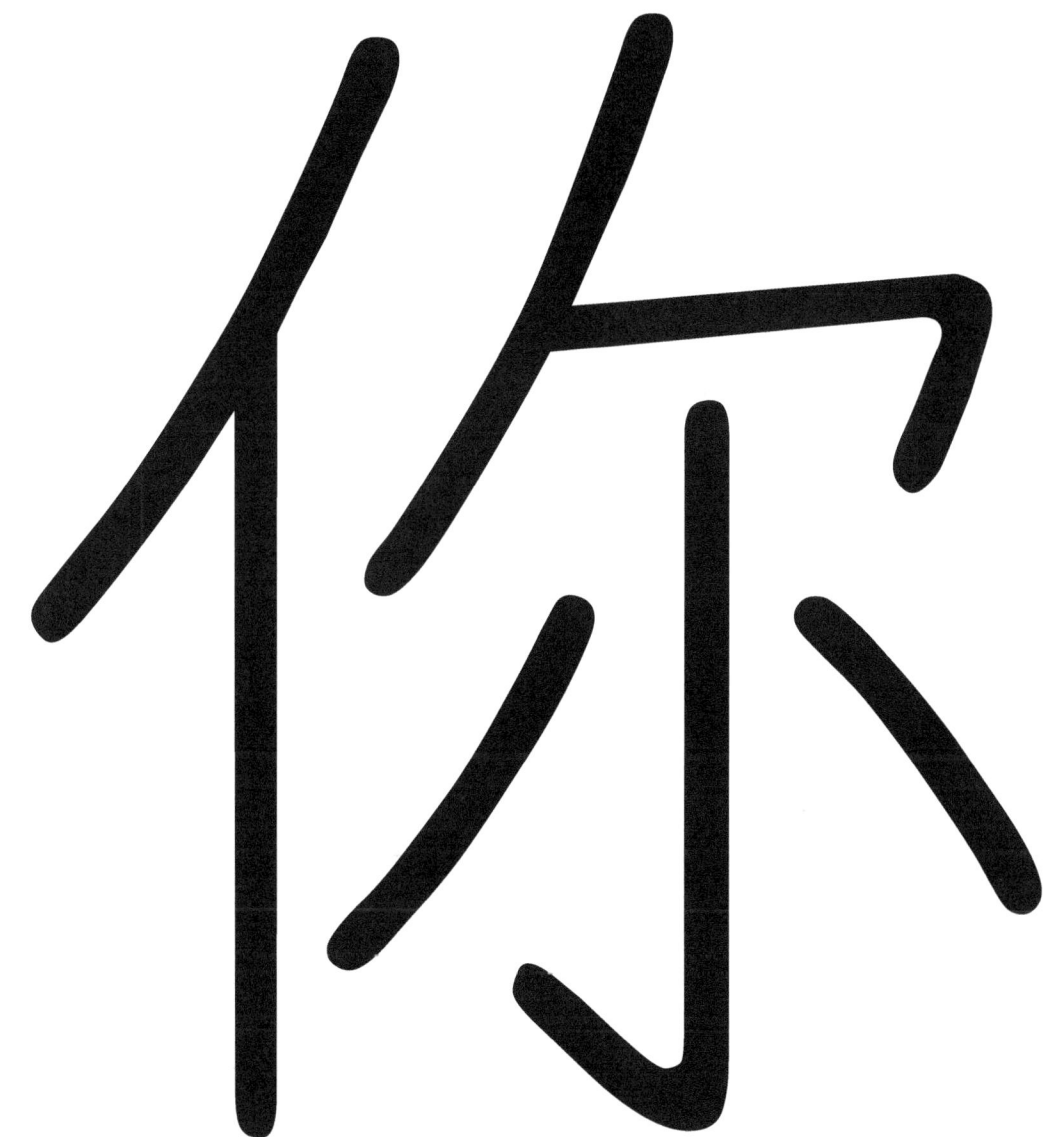

Describe your picture and write how you will remember what the character means and what it sounds like:

你

Simplified

nǐ
you

你

Traditional

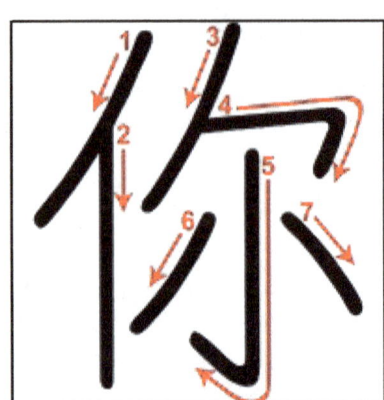

你 nǐ *you*

你们 nǐmen* *you-all*

你好 nǐhǎo *How are you?; Hello.*

迷你 mǐnǐ *mini, micro*

Strokes: 7

Radical: 亻（人）réN
    'person'

Pinyin: nǐ

Practice writing this character using the stroke order shown above.
When you're finished, circle the one that you like the best.

你 你 你 你 你 你

你 你 你 你 你 你 你 你

My Character Picture for

niáN   year

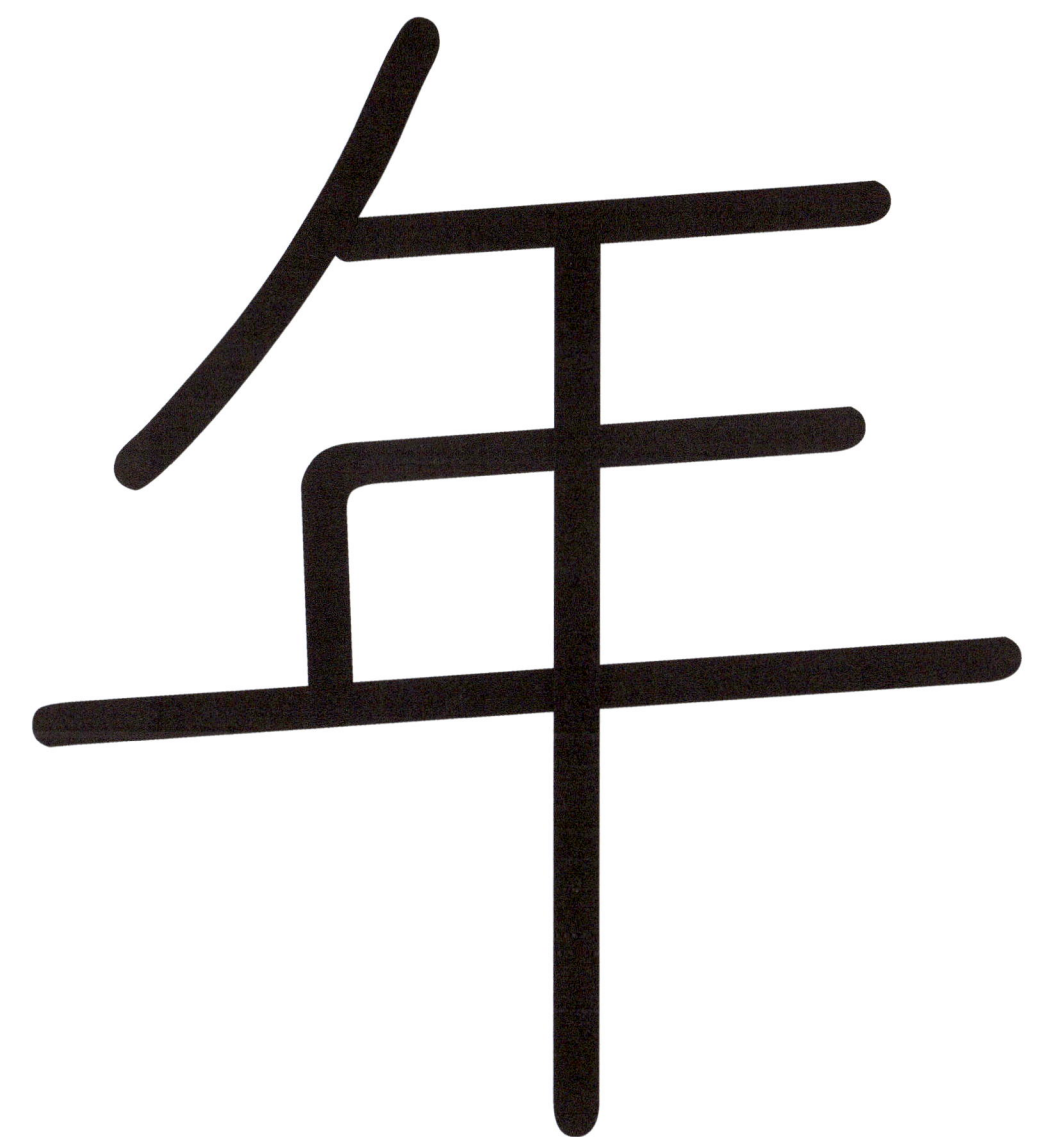

Describe your picture and write how you will remember what the character means and what it sounds like:

Simplified

niáN

year

Traditional

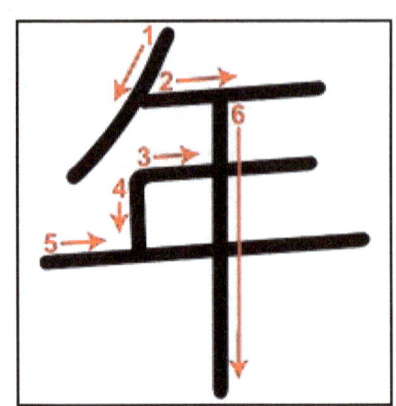

年 niáN *year*

今年 JĪNniáN *this year*

去年 QùniáN *last year*

青年 QĪNGniáN *youth*

年轻 niáNQĪNG *young*

Strokes: 6

Radical: 干 GĀN
　　　　'to do'

Pinyin: nián

Practice writing this character using the stroke order shown above.
When you're finished, circle the one that you like the best.

年	年	年	年	年	年

年 年 年 年 年 年 年 年

My Character Picture for
nǚ *female*

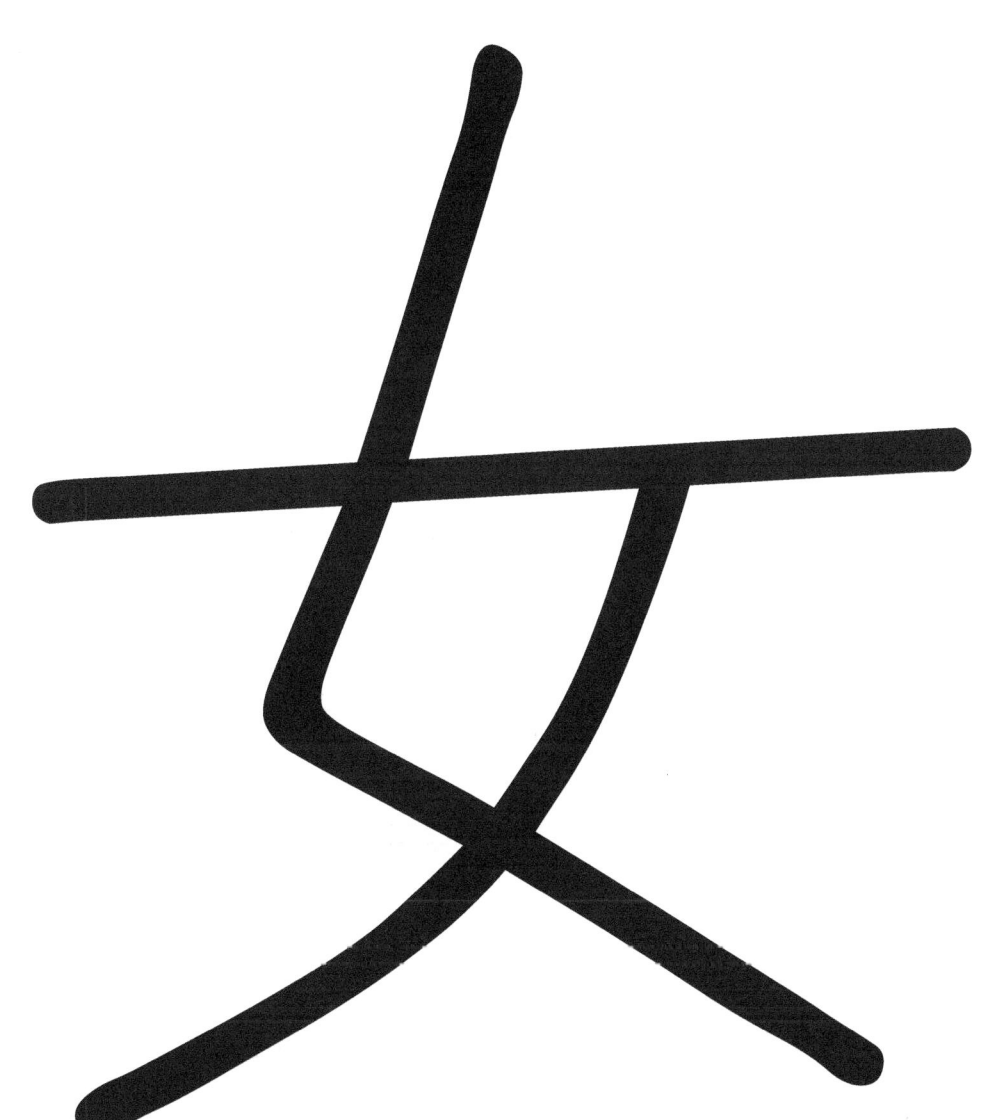

Describe your picture and write how you will remember what the character means and what it sounds like:

女

Simplified

nǚ

female

女

Traditional

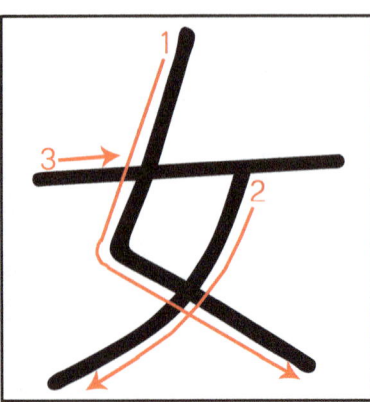

女人 nǚréN *woman*

女孩 nǚháI *girl*

女厕所 nǚCèsuǒ *women's toilet*

女儿 nǚ'éR *daughter*

男女 náN-nǚ *men and women*

Strokes: 3

Radical: 女 nǚ *'woman'*

Pinyin: nǚ

Practice writing this character using the stroke order shown above.
When you're finished, circle the one that you like the best.

女 女 女 女 女 女

女 女 女 女 女 女 女 女

My Character Picture for

pénG *friend*

Describe your picture and write how you will remember what the character means and what it sounds like:

朋

Simplified

pénG
friend

朋

Traditional

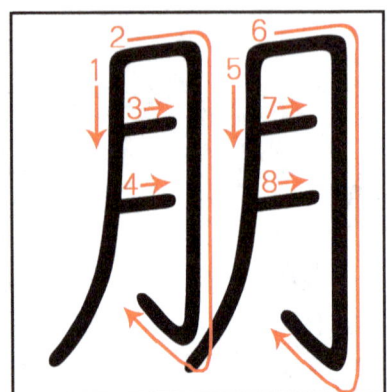

朋友　pénGyou*　*friend*

小朋友　xiǎopénGyou*　*children*

女朋友　nǚpénGyou*　*girlfriend*

男朋友　náNpénGyou*　*boyfriend*

Strokes: 8

Radical: 月 Yuè '*moon*'

Pinyin: péng

Practice writing this character using the stroke order shown above.
When you're finished, circle the one that you like the best.

朋　朋　朋　朋　朋　朋

My Character Picture for

QĪ *a period of time*

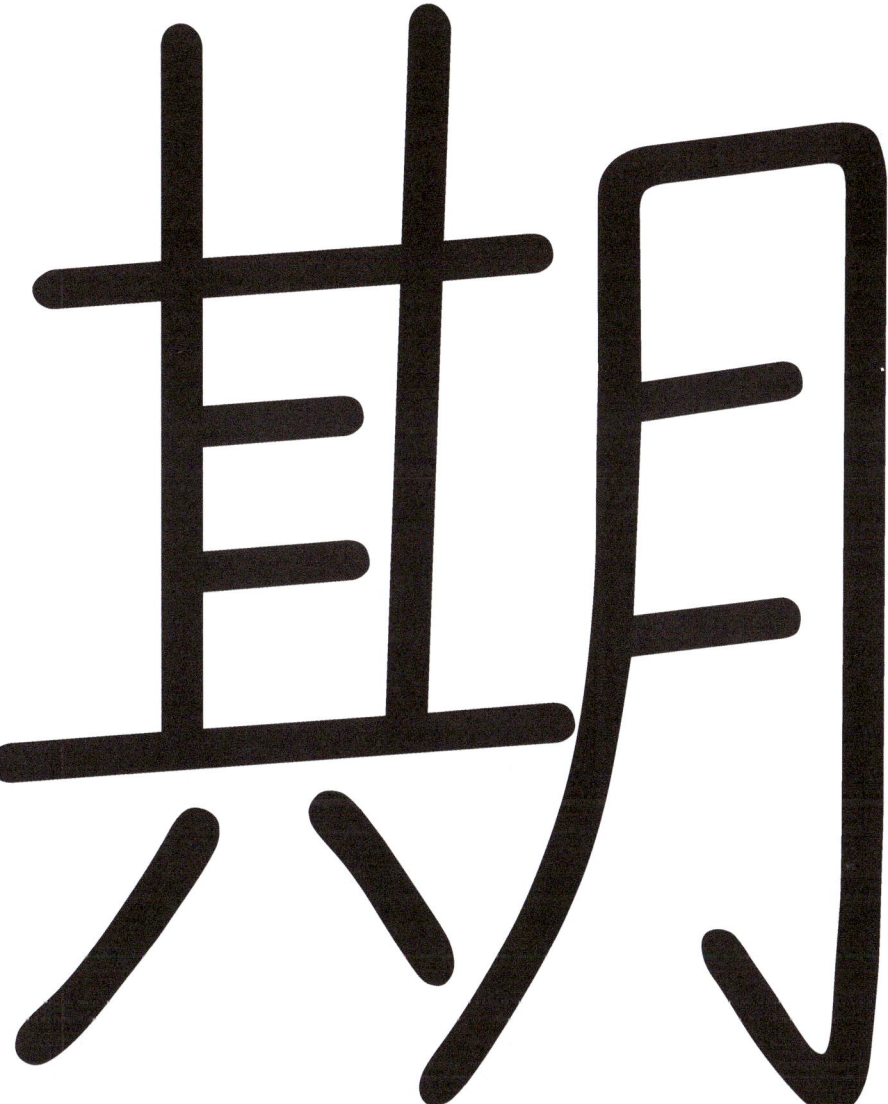

Describe your picture and write how you will remember what the character means and what it sounds like:

期

Simplified

QĪ

a period of time

期

Traditional

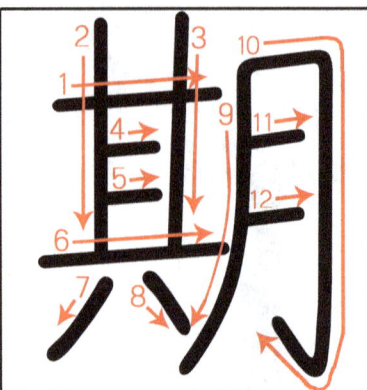

星期　XĪNGQĪ　*week*

日期　RìQĪ　*date*

时期　shíQĪ　*a period in time or history*

长期　chánGQĪ　*long term*

星期一　XĪNGQĪYĪ　*Monday*

Strokes: 12

Radical: 月 Yuè '*moon*'

Pinyin: qī

Practice writing this character using the stroke order shown above.
When you're finished, circle the one that you like the best.

期	期	期	期	期	期

期 期 期 期 期 期 期 期 期

My Character Picture for

Qì air

Describe your picture and write how you will remember what the character means and what it sounds like:

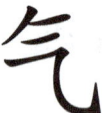

名字＿＿＿＿＿＿＿＿＿＿＿＿ ＿＿＿＿年 ＿＿＿月 ＿＿＿日

气 Qì 氣

Simplified — air — Traditional

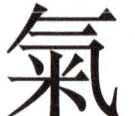

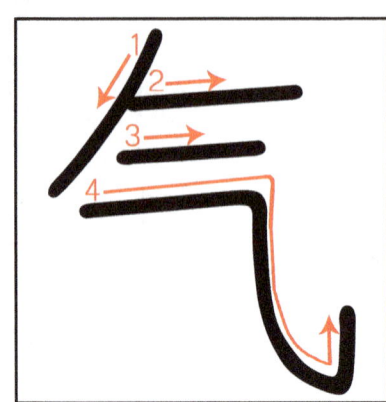

气 Qì *air*

天气 TIĀNQì *weather*

生气 SHĒNGQì *angry*

空气 KŌNGQì *air, atmosphere*

客气 Kèqi* *polite*

Strokes: 4

Radical: 气 Qì *'air'*

Pinyin: qì

Practice writing this character using the stroke order shown above.
When you're finished, circle the one that you like the best.

气	气	气	气	气	气

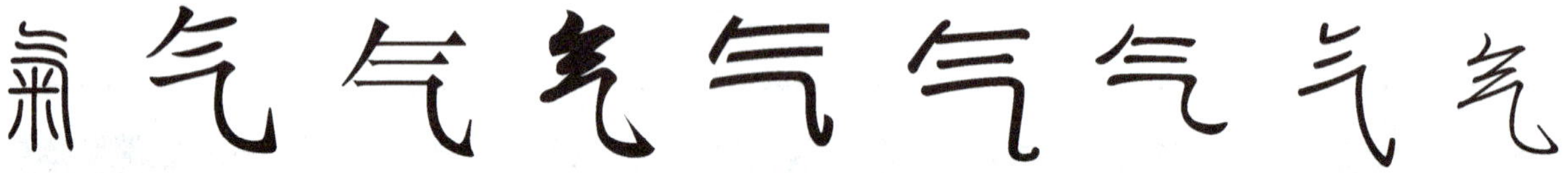

My Character Picture for

qǐng *ask/please*

请

Describe your picture and write how you will remember what the character means and what it sounds like:

请

Simplified

qǐng

ask / please

請

Traditional

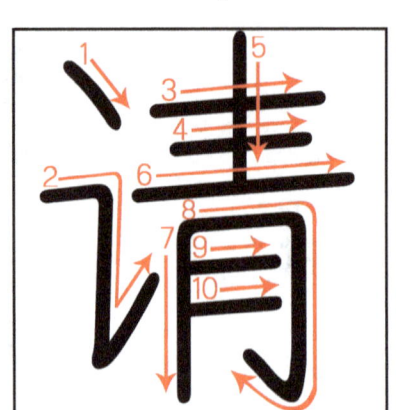

请　qǐng　*please*

请问　qǐngWèn　*may I ask*

请坐　qǐngZuò　*please sit down*

请客　qǐngKè　*invite guests*

请勿　qǐngWù　*please don't…*
　　　　　　(on signs)

Strokes: 10

Radical: 讠 (言) yáN
　　　　　'speech'

Pinyin: qǐng

Practice writing this character using the stroke order shown above.
When you're finished, circle the one that you like the best.

My Character Picture for
Qù *go*

Describe your picture and write how you will remember what the character means and what it sounds like:

去
Simplified

Qù
go

去
Traditional

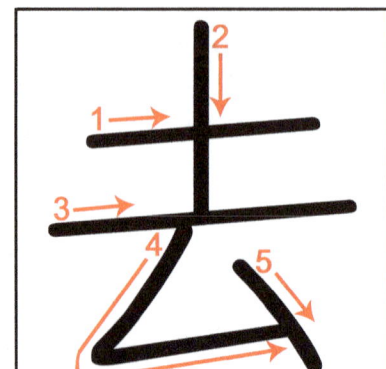

去 Qù *go*

下去 Xiàqu* *go down*

出去 CHŪqu* *go out*

去年 QùniáN *last year*

进去 Jìnqu* *go in*

Strokes: 5

Radical: 厶 SĪ
'private'

Pinyin: qù

Practice writing this character using the stroke order shown above.
When you're finished, circle the one that you like the best.

My Character Picture for

ráN   *correct/right*

Describe your picture and write how you will remember what the character means and what it sounds like:

然
Simplified

ráN
correct / right

然
Traditional

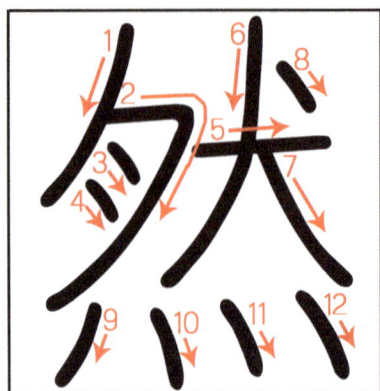

虽然 SUĪráN *although*

忽然 HŪráN *suddenly*

当然 DĀNGráN *certainly*

自然 ZìráN *natural world*

然后 ráNHòu *and then*

Strokes: 12

Radical: ⺍ (火) huǒ 'fire'

Pinyin: rán

Practice writing this character using the stroke order shown above.
When you're finished, circle the one that you like the best.

My Character Picture for
réN   man/person/people

Describe your picture and write how you will remember what the character means and what it sounds like:

人

Simplified

réN

man / person / people

人 **Traditional**

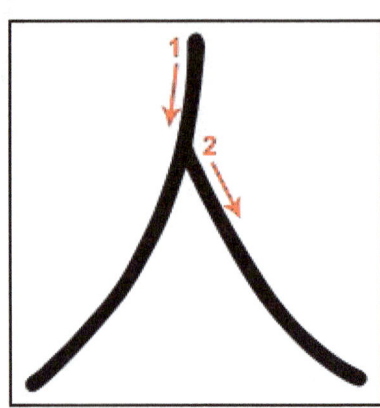

人 réN *person*

女人 nǚréN *woman*

男人 náNréN *man*

人民 réNmíN *the people*

别人 biÉréN *other people*

Strokes: 2

Radical: 人 réN
'*person*'

Pinyin: rén

*Practice writing this character using the stroke order shown above.
When you're finished, circle the one that you like the best.*

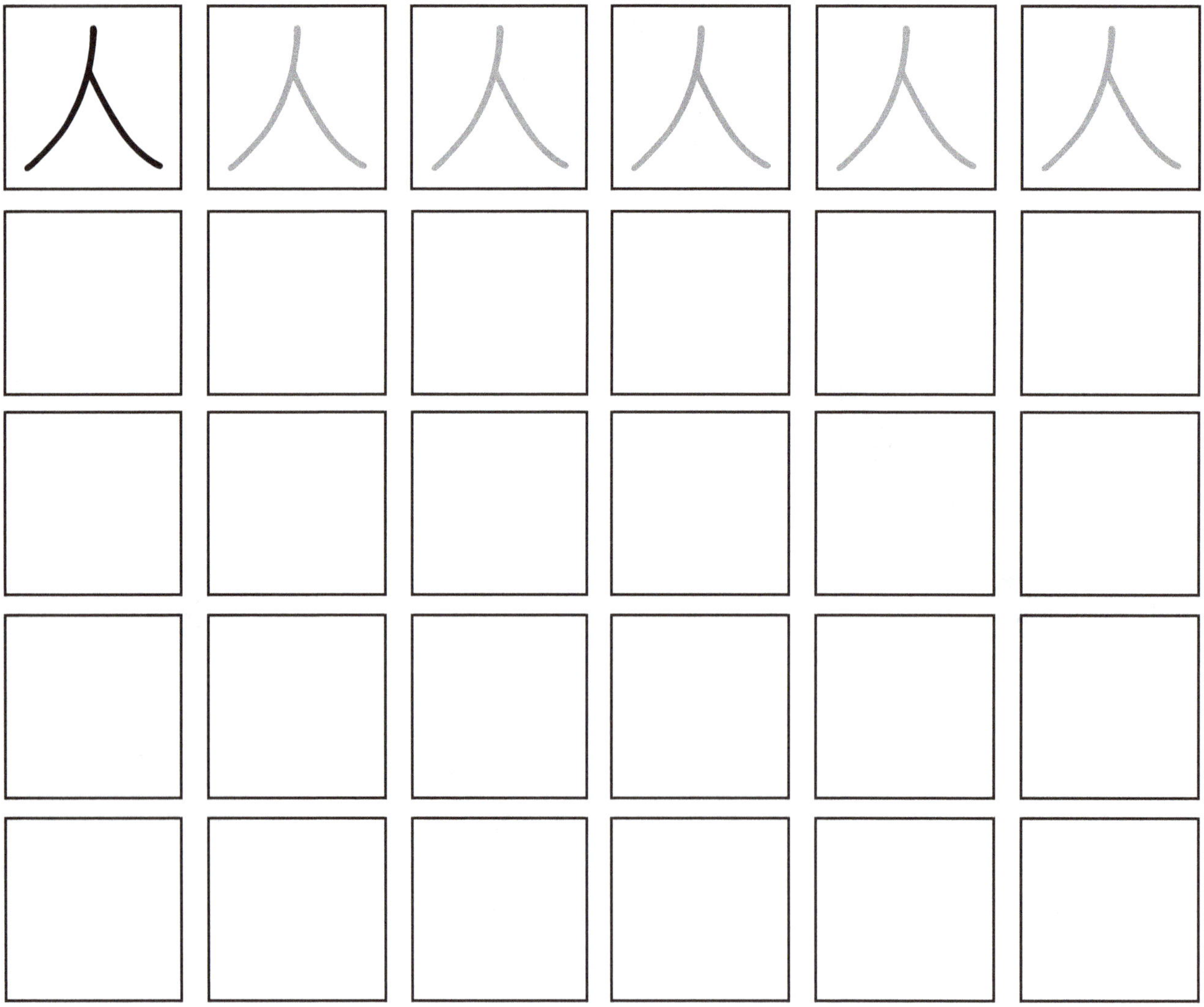

My Character Picture for
Rì   *sun, day*

Describe your picture and write how you will remember what the character means and what it sounds like:

名字________________________________ ________年 _____月 _____日

日 Rì 日

Simplified — sun, day — Traditional

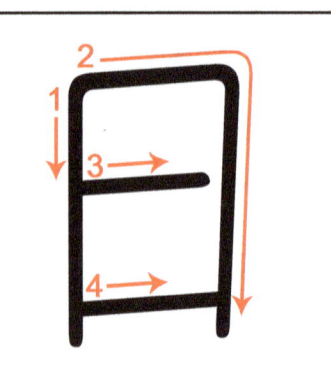

日 Rì *sun*

生日 SHĒNGRì *birthday*

日子 Rìzi* *day, life*

日记 RìJì *diary, journal*

节日 jiÉRì *holiday, festival*

Strokes: 4

Radical: 日 Rì *'sun'*

Pinyin: rì

Practice writing this character using the stroke order shown above.
When you're finished, circle the one that you like the best.

日	日	日	日	日	日

日 日 日 日 日 日 日 日 日

My Character Picture for

rÚ   *if / be like*

如

Describe your picture and write how you will remember what the character means and what it sounds like:

如

Simplified

rÚ

if / be like

如

Traditional

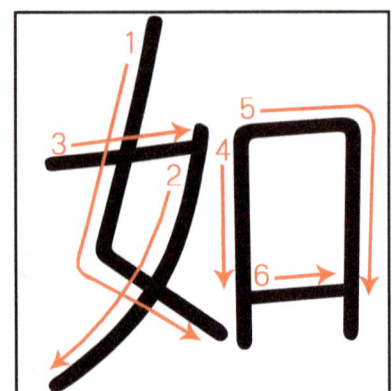

如果 rÚguǒ *if*

如何 rÚhÉ *how; how about it?*

如此 rÚcǐ *like this; thus*

Strokes: 6

Radical: 女 nü *'woman'*

Pinyin: rú

Practice writing this character using the stroke order shown above.
When you're finished, circle the one that you like the best.

如 如 如 如 如 如

如 如 如 如 如 如 如

My Character Picture for
shǎo *few / less*

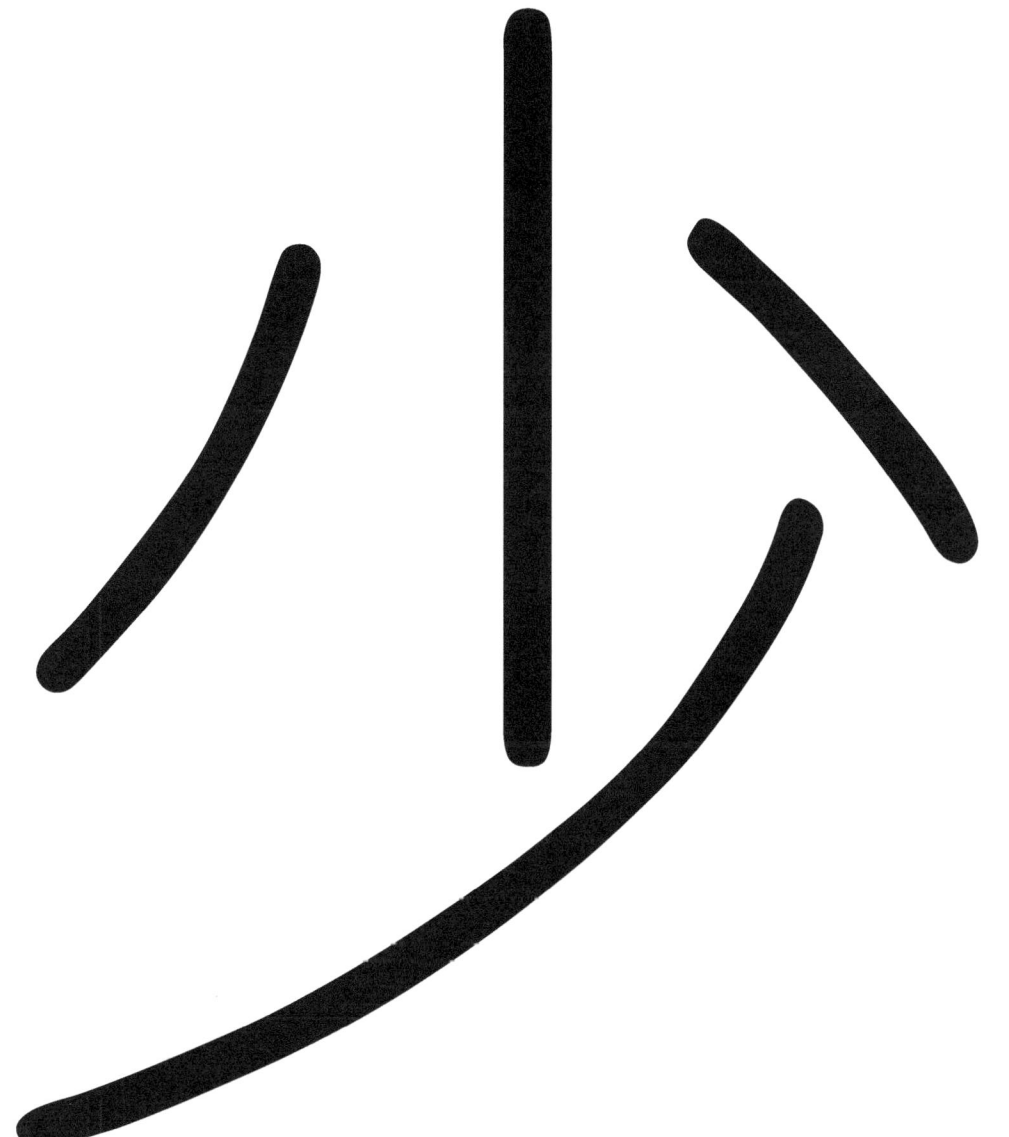

Describe your picture and write how you will remember what the character means and what it sounds like:

少

Simplified

shǎo

few / less

少

Traditional

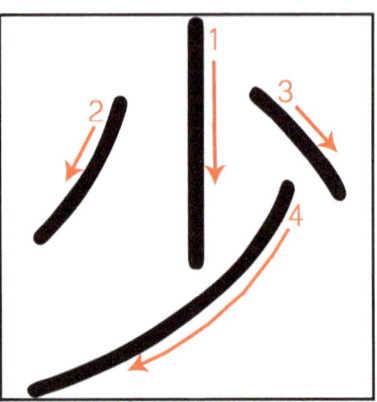

多 少　DUŌshǎo　*how many;*
how much?

不 少　Bùshǎo　*many; not few*

最 少　Zuìshǎo　*least; minimum*

太 少　Tàishǎo　*too little; few*

少 数　shǎoShù　*a small number;*
minority

Strokes: 4

Radical: 小 xiǎo *'small'*

Pinyin: shǎo

Practice writing this character using the stroke order shown above.
When you're finished, circle the one that you like the best.

少　少　少　少　少　少

少　少　少　少　少　少　少　少

My Character Picture for

shéI *who*

Describe your picture and write how you will remember what the character means and what it sounds like:

谁
Simplified

shéI
who

誰
Traditional

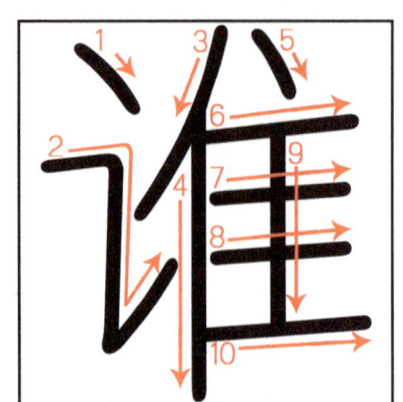

谁 shéI *who?*

是 谁 Shì shéI *who is it?*

谁 的 shéIde* *whose?*

Strokes: 10

Radical: 讠 (言) yáN
'*speech*'

Pinyin: shéi

*Practice writing this character using the stroke order shown above.
When you're finished, circle the one that you like the best.*

My Character Picture for
shéN   *what*

Describe your picture and write how you will remember what the character means and what it sounds like:

＿＿＿＿＿＿＿＿＿＿＿＿＿＿＿＿＿＿＿＿＿＿＿＿＿＿＿＿＿＿＿＿＿＿

＿＿＿＿＿＿＿＿＿＿＿＿＿＿＿＿＿＿＿＿＿＿＿＿＿＿＿＿＿＿＿＿＿＿

＿＿＿＿＿＿＿＿＿＿＿＿＿＿＿＿＿＿＿＿＿＿＿＿＿＿＿＿＿＿＿＿＿＿

名字______________________________ ________年 _____月 _____日

什 shéN 甚

Simplified — what — Traditional

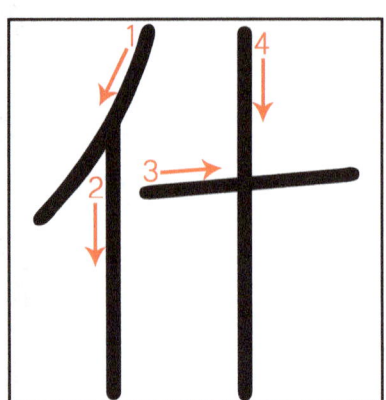

什么 shéNme* *what?*

为什么 WèishéNme* *why?*

没什么 méI shéNme* *never mind*

什么的 shéNme* de* *and so on*

什么时候 shéNme* shÍHòu *when?*

Strokes: 4

Radical: 亻 (人) réN *'person'*

Pinyin: shén

Practice writing this character using the stroke order shown above. When you're finished, circle the one that you like the best.

什 什 什 什 什 什

什 什 什 什 什 什 什 什 什

My Character Picture for

SHĒNG   *to be born/life/to grow*

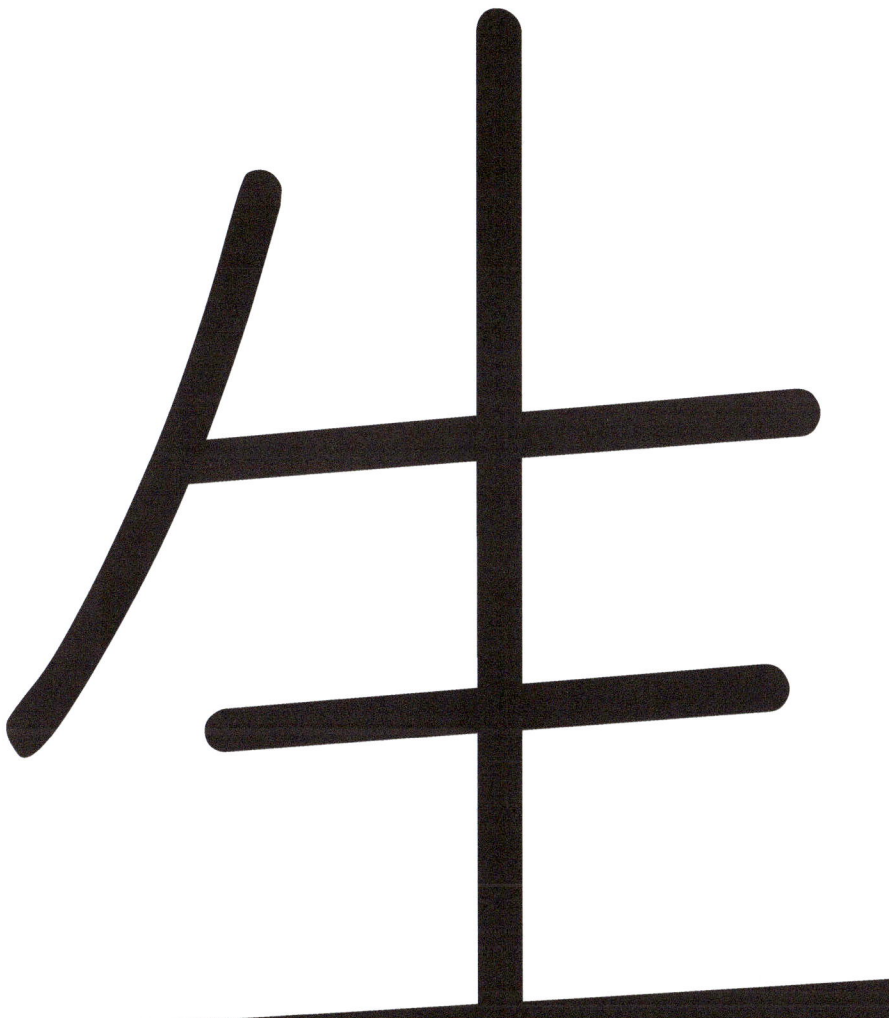

Describe your picture and write how you will remember what the character means and what it sounds like:

SHĒNG

to be born / life / to grow

生 Simplified

生 Traditional

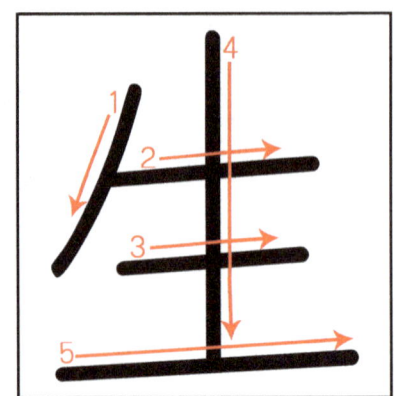

学生 xuÉSHĒNG *student*

生活 SHĒNGhuÓ *life*

先生 XIĀNsheng* *Mr., sir*

生日 SHĒNGRì *birthday*

医生 YĪSHĒNG *doctor*

Strokes: 5

Radical: 生 SHĒNG 'life'

Pinyin: shēng

Practice writing this character using the stroke order shown above.
When you're finished, circle the one that you like the best.

生	生	生	生	生	生

生 生 生 生 生 生 生 生 生

My Character Picture for
shí   time

Describe your picture and write how you will remember what the character means and what it sounds like:

时

Simplified

shí

time

時

Traditional

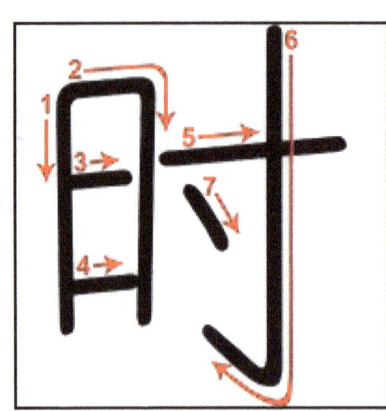

时候 shíhou* *moment in time*

时间 shíJIĀN *time*

当时 DĀNGshí *at that time*

有时候 yǒushíhou* *sometimes*

小时 xiǎoshí *hour*

Strokes: 7

Radical: 日 Rì *'the sun'*

Pinyin: shí

*Practice writing this character using the stroke order shown above.
When you're finished, circle the one that you like the best.*

时　时　时　时　时　时

时 时 时 时 时 时 时 时

My Character Picture for
Shì   is/are/am/yes/to be

Describe your picture and write how you will remember what the character means and what it sounds like:

是
Simplified

Shì

is / are / am / yes / to be

是
Traditional

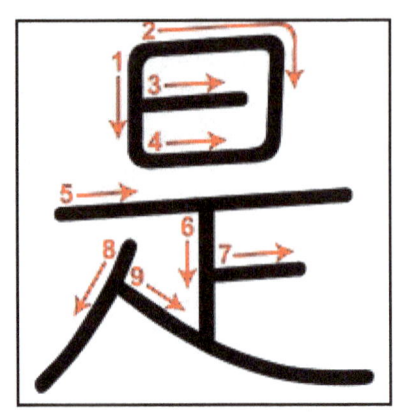

是 Shì *is, are, am*

可是 kěShì *but*

但是 DànShì *but*

还是 háIShì *or*

是的 Shìde* *yes (emphatic)*

Strokes: 9

Radical: 日 Rì '*sun*'

Pinyin: shì

Practice writing this character using the stroke order shown above.
When you're finished, circle the one that you like the best.

是　是　是　是　是　是

是 是 是 是 是 是 是 是 是

My Character Picture for
SHŪ   book

Describe your picture and write how you will remember what the character means and what it sounds like:

＿＿＿＿＿＿＿＿＿＿＿＿＿＿＿＿＿＿＿＿＿＿＿＿＿＿＿＿＿＿

＿＿＿＿＿＿＿＿＿＿＿＿＿＿＿＿＿＿＿＿＿＿＿＿＿＿＿＿＿＿

＿＿＿＿＿＿＿＿＿＿＿＿＿＿＿＿＿＿＿＿＿＿＿＿＿＿＿＿＿＿

书
Simplified

SHŪ
book

書
Traditional

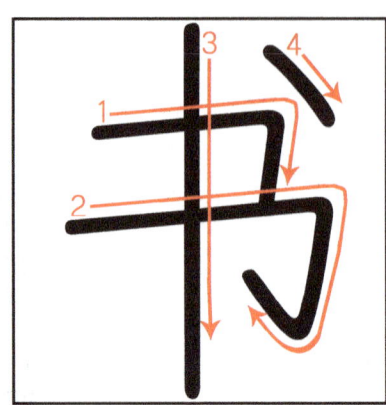

书 SHŪ *book*

图书馆 tÚSHŪguǎn *library*

读书 dÚSHŪ *read*

书店 SHŪDiàn *bookstore*

书法 SHŪfǎ *calligraphy*

Strokes: 4

Radical: 一 (乙) Yî
'second'

Pinyin: shū

Practice writing this character using the stroke order shown above.
When you're finished, circle the one that you like the best.

名字＿＿＿＿＿＿＿＿＿＿＿＿＿ ＿＿＿年 ＿＿月 ＿＿日

My Character Picture for
SHUŌ   to speak/to say

Describe your picture and write how you will remember what the character means and what it sounds like:

SHUŌ

to speak / to say

说　Simplified

說　Traditional

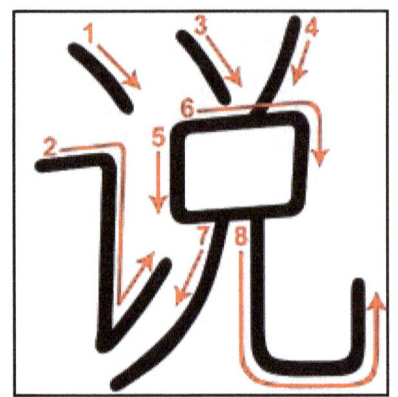

说　SHUŌ　*speak; talk*

说话　SHUŌHuà　*speak; talk; chat*

听说　TĪNGSHUŌ　*hear it said that*

就是说　JìuShìSHUŌ　*that is to say*

小说　xiǎoSHUŌ　*novel; fiction*

Strokes: 8

Radical: 讠(言) yáN
　　　　'speech'

Pinyin: shuō

Practice writing this character using the stroke order shown above.
When you're finished, circle the one that you like the best.

说　说　说　说　说　说

说 说 说 说 说 说 说 说

My Character Picture for
SUĪ   *though*

Describe your picture and write how you will remember what the character means and what it sounds like:

虽
Simplified

SUĪ
though

雞
Traditional

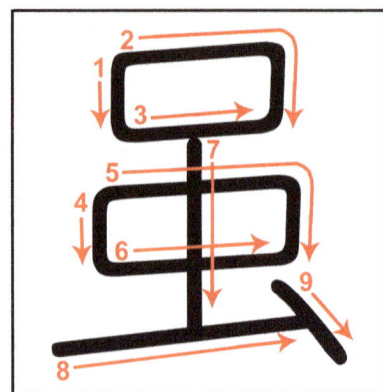

虽然 SUĪráN *although*

Strokes: 9

Radical: 虫 chónG
'insect'

Pinyin: suī

Practice writing this character using the stroke order shown above.
When you're finished, circle the one that you like the best.

虽 虽 虽 虽 虽 虽

雞 虽 虽 虽 虽 虽 虽 虽 虽

My Character Picture for

Suì   *age/year*

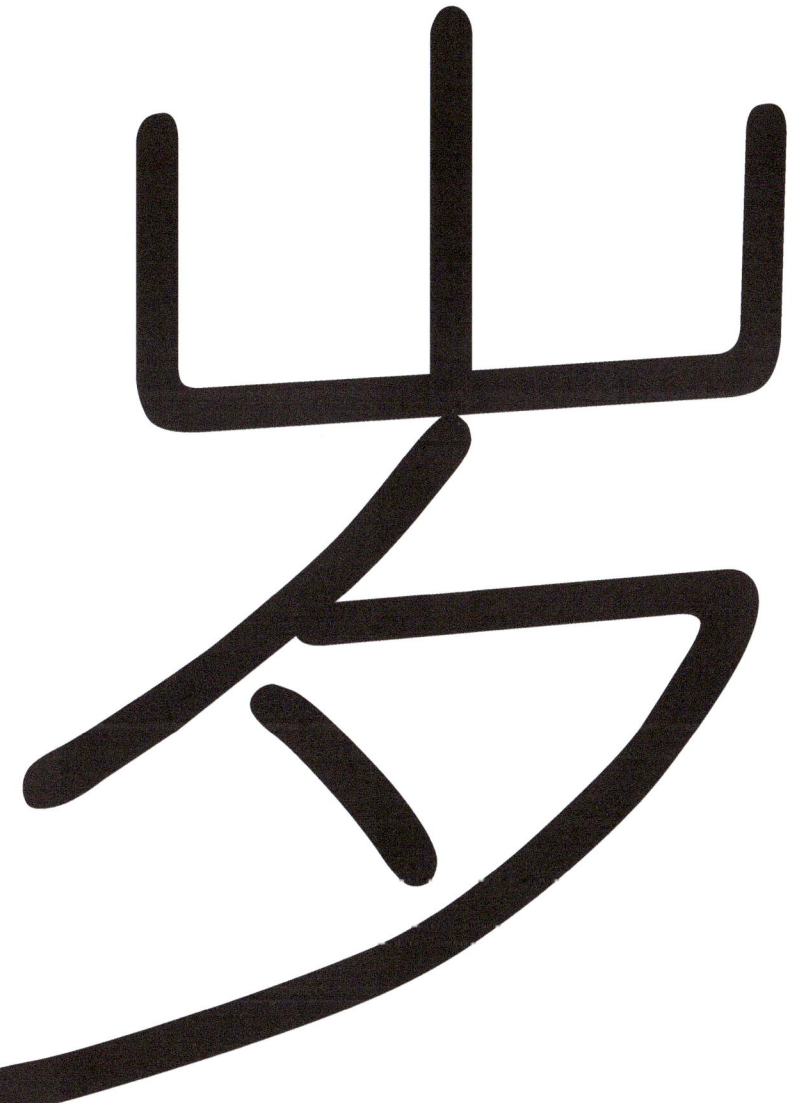

Describe your picture and write how you will remember what the character means and what it sounds like:

\--

\--

\--

岁

Simplified

Suì

age / year

歲

Traditional

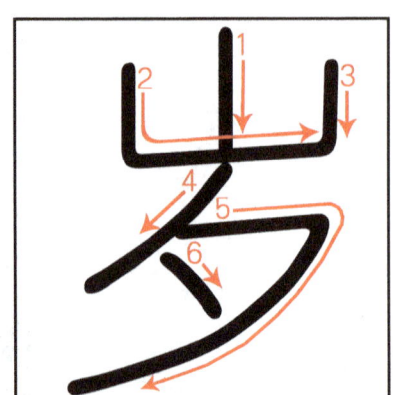

几 岁　jǐSuì　*how old?*

十 岁　shí Suì　*ten years old*

万 岁　WànSuì　*long life (10,00 years)*

Strokes: 6

Radical: 山 SHĀN
'mountain'

Pinyin: suī

Practice writing this character using the stroke order shown above.
When you're finished, circle the one that you like the best.

My Character Picture for
suǒ   *actually/place*

所

Describe your picture and write how you will remember what the character means and what it sounds like:

＿＿＿＿＿＿＿＿＿＿＿＿＿＿＿＿＿＿＿＿＿＿＿＿＿＿

＿＿＿＿＿＿＿＿＿＿＿＿＿＿＿＿＿＿＿＿＿＿＿＿＿＿

＿＿＿＿＿＿＿＿＿＿＿＿＿＿＿＿＿＿＿＿＿＿＿＿＿＿

所

Simplified

suǒ

actually / place

所

Traditional

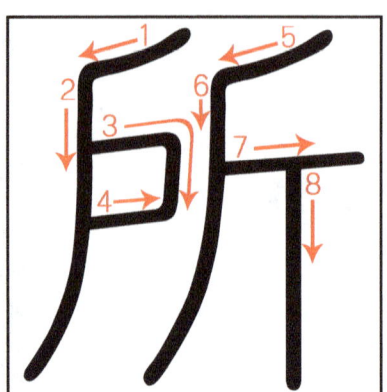

所以　suǒyǐ　*so, therefore*

所有　suǒyǒu　*all, every*

厕所　Cèsuǒ　*toilet*

所谓　suǒWèi　*so-called*

Strokes: 8

Radical: 戶 Hù *'door'*

Pinyin: suǒ

Practice writing this character using the stroke order shown above.
When you're finished, circle the one that you like the best.

My Character Picture for
TĀ *he/him*

Describe your picture and write how you will remember what the character means and what it sounds like:

他
Simplified

TĀ
he / him

他
Traditional

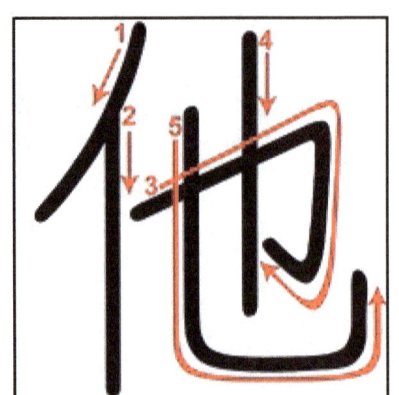

他 TĀ *he, him*
他们 TĀmen* *they*
其他 qíTĀ *other*
吉他 jíta* *guitar*

Strokes: 5
Radical: 亻(人) réN
 'person'
Pinyin: tā

Practice writing this character using the stroke order shown above.
When you're finished, circle the one that you like the best.

他 他 他 他 他 他

他 他 他 他 他 他 他

My Character Picture for

TĀ *she/her*

Describe your picture and write how you will remember what the character means and what it sounds like:

她
Simplified

TĀ
she / her

她
Traditional

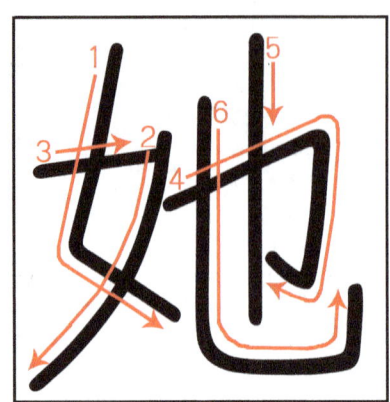

她 TĀ *she, her*

她们 TĀmen* *they (female)*

她的 TĀde* *hers*

Strokes: 6

Radical: 女 nǚ *'woman'*

Pinyin: tā

Practice writing this character using the stroke order shown above.
When you're finished, circle the one that you like the best.

My Character Picture for
TIĀN *sky, heaven, day*

Describe your picture and write how you will remember what the character means and what it sounds like:

TIĀN

sky, heaven, day

天
Simplified

天
Traditional

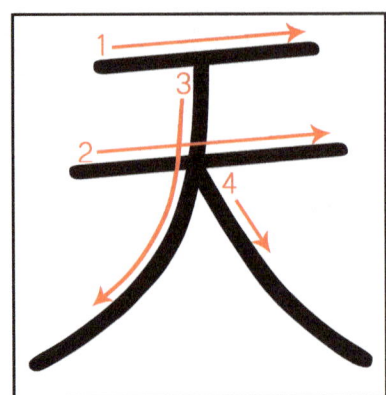

今天 JĪNTIĀN *today*

明天 mínGTIĀN *tomorrow*

昨天 zuÓTIĀN *yesterday*

春天 CHŪNTIĀN *springtime*

天气 TIĀNQì *weather*

Strokes: 4

Radical: 大 Dà 'big'

Pinyin: tiān

Practice writing this character using the stroke order shown above.
When you're finished, circle the one that you like the best.

My Character Picture for
tiáO   strip / (measure word for long, narrow things)

Describe your picture and write how you will remember what the character means and what it sounds like:

条
Simplified

tiáO
strip /
(measure word for long, narrow things)

條
Traditional

面条　MiàntiáO　*noodles*

枝条　ZHĪtiáO　*branch, twig*

油条　yóUtiáO　*deep-fried twisted dough sticks*

薯条　shǔtiáO　*french fries*

Strokes: 7

Radical: 木 Mù *'tree'*

Pinyin: tiáo

*Practice writing this character using the stroke order shown above.
When you're finished, circle the one that you like the best.*

条　条　条　条　条　条

條 条 条 条 条 条 条 条

My Character Picture for
tóU   *head*

Describe your picture and write how you will remember what the character means and what it sounds like:

\-

\-

\-

头
Simplified

tóU
head

頭
Traditional

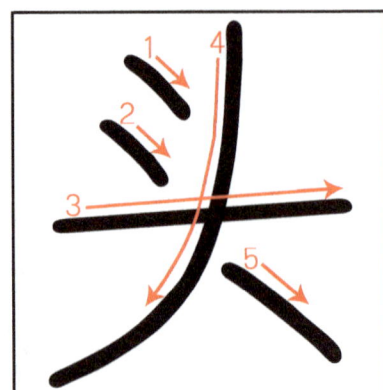

头 tóu *head*

头发 tóufa* *hair*

石头 shÍtou* *rock*

点头 DiàntóU *nod*

头痛 tóUTòng *headache*

Strokes: 5

Radical: 大 Dà *'big'*

Pinyin: tóu

Practice writing this character using the stroke order shown above.
When you're finished, circle the one that you like the best.

My Character Picture for

wéI / Wèi   *for/on account of*

Describe your picture and write how you will remember what the character means and what it sounds like:

为

Simplified

wéI / Wèi

for / on account of

為

Traditional

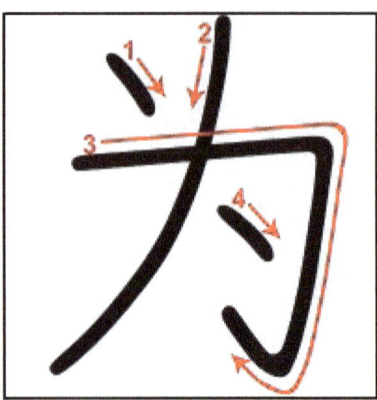

因为　YĪNWèi　*because*

为了　Wèile*　*in order to*

为什么　WèishéNme*　*why?*

以为　yǐwéI *believe falsely that*

认为　Rènwéi　*think, consider*

Strokes: 4

Radical: 丶 zhÚ *'dot'*

Pinyin: wéi / wèi

Practice writing this character using the stroke order shown above.
When you're finished, circle the one that you like the best.

为　为　为　为　为　为

为　为　为　为　为　为　为

My Character Picture for
wéN language/culture/writing

Describe your picture and write how you will remember what the character means and what it sounds like:

文
Simplified

wéN

language / culture / writing

文
Traditional

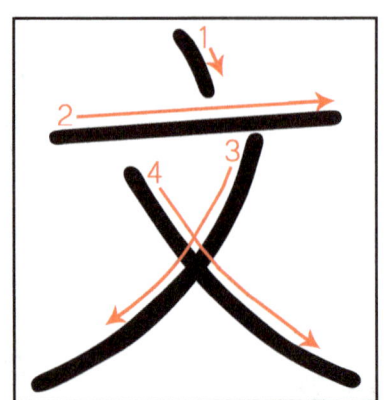

英文　YĪNGwéN　*English*

文化　wéNHuà　*culture*

文字　wéNZì　*character*

文学　wéNxuÉ　*literature*

中文　ZHŌNGwéN　*Chinese language*

Strokes: 4

Radical: 文 wéN
　　　　'script'

Pinyin: wén

Practice writing this character using the stroke order shown above.
When you're finished, circle the one that you like the best.

文　文　文　文　文　文

文 文 文 文 文 文 文 文

My Character Picture for
wǒ   I/me/myself

Describe your picture and write how you will remember what the character means and what it sounds like:

名字＿＿＿＿＿＿＿＿＿＿＿＿＿＿＿＿＿＿ ＿＿年 ＿＿月 ＿＿日

我
Simplified

wǒ
I / me / myself

我
Traditional

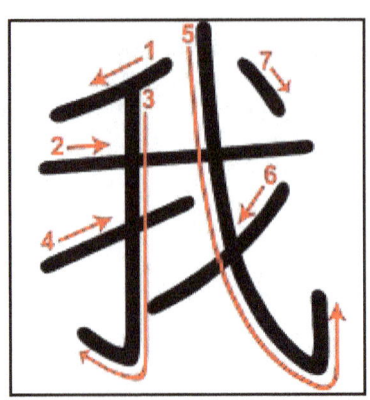

我　wǒ　*I*
我 们　wǒmen*　*we*
我 的　wǒde*　*my*
我 们 的　wǒmen*de*　*ours*

Strokes: 7
Radical: 戈 GĒ *'a spear'*
Pinyin: wǒ

Practice writing this character using the stroke order shown above.
When you're finished, circle the one that you like the best.

我 | 我 | 我 | 我 | 我 | 我

我 我 我 我 我 我 我 我

My Character Picture for
xǐ   *like/fond of/happy*

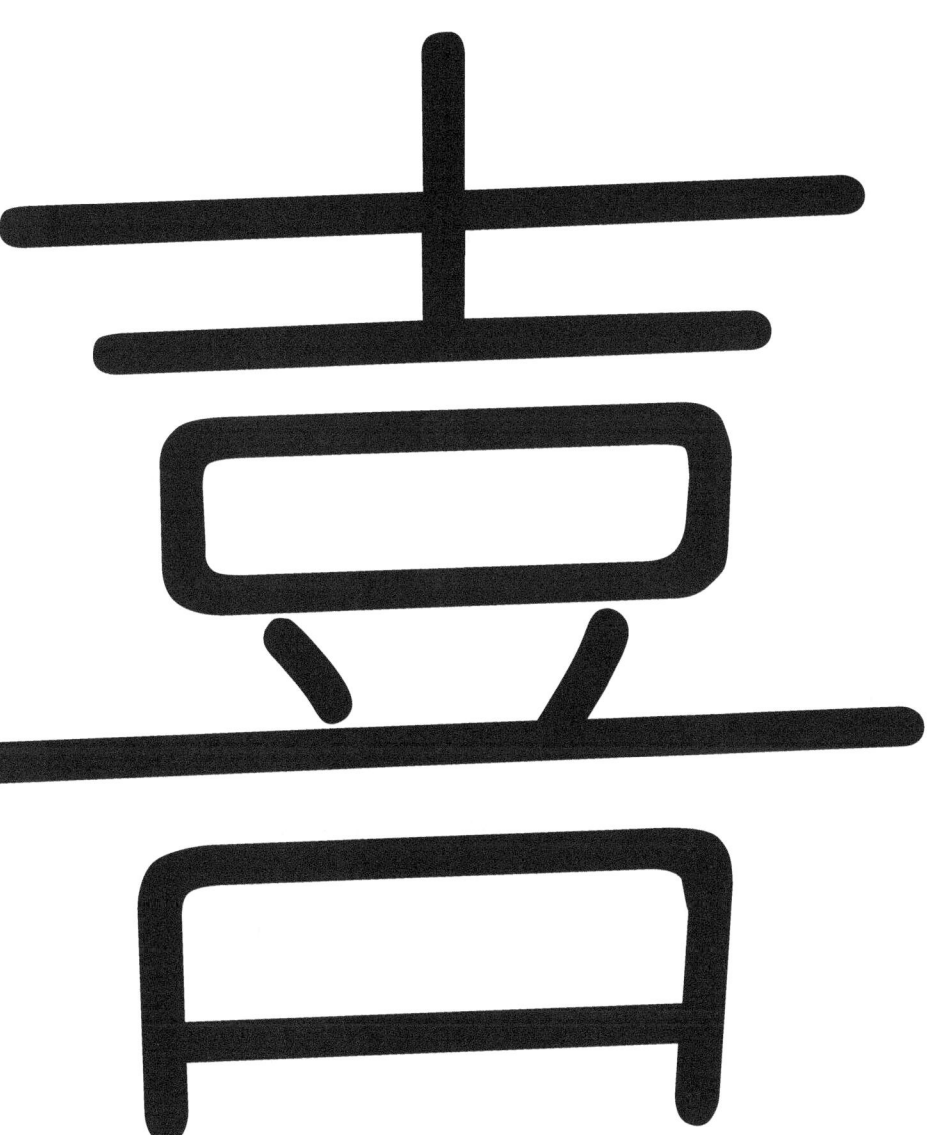

Describe your picture and write how you will remember what the character means and what it sounds like:

喜
Simplified

xǐ
like / fond of / happy

喜
Traditional

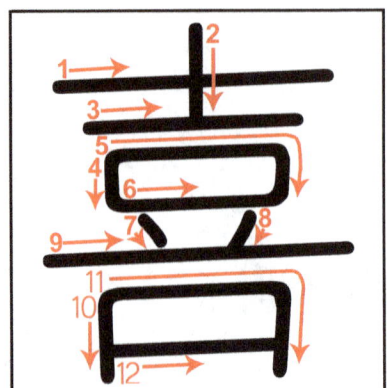

喜 xǐ *like, be fond of*

喜欢 xǐHUĀN *like*

欢喜 HUĀNxǐ *like, be fond of*

喜爱 xǐ'Ài *like, love*

惊喜 JĪNGxǐ *pleasantly surprised*

Strokes: 12

Radical: 口 kǒu
  'mouth'

Pinyin: xǐ

Practice writing this character using the stroke order shown above.
When you're finished, circle the one that you like the best.

喜　喜　喜　喜　喜　喜

喜 喜 喜 喜 喜 喜 喜 喜

My Character Picture for
xiǎng   *wants to/think*

Describe your picture and write how you will remember what the character means and what it sounds like:

想

Simplified

xiǎng

wants to / think

想

Traditional

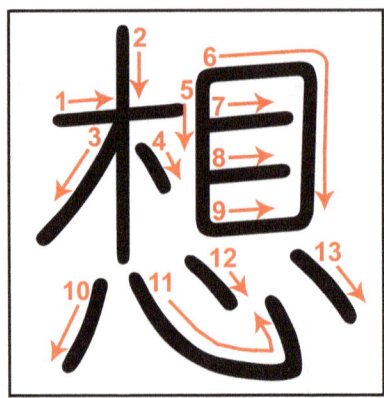

想 xiǎng *think*

想吃 xiǎngCHĪ *wants to eat*

思想 SĪxiǎng *thought*

想一想 xiǎngYĪxiǎng *think about it*

没想到 méI xiǎngDào

have not thought of

Strokes: 13

Radical: 心 XĪN *'heart'*

Pinyin: xiǎng

Practice writing this character using the stroke order shown above.
When you're finished, circle the one that you like the best.

想　想　想　想　想　想

想 想 想 想 想 想 想 想

My Character Picture for
XĪNG *star*

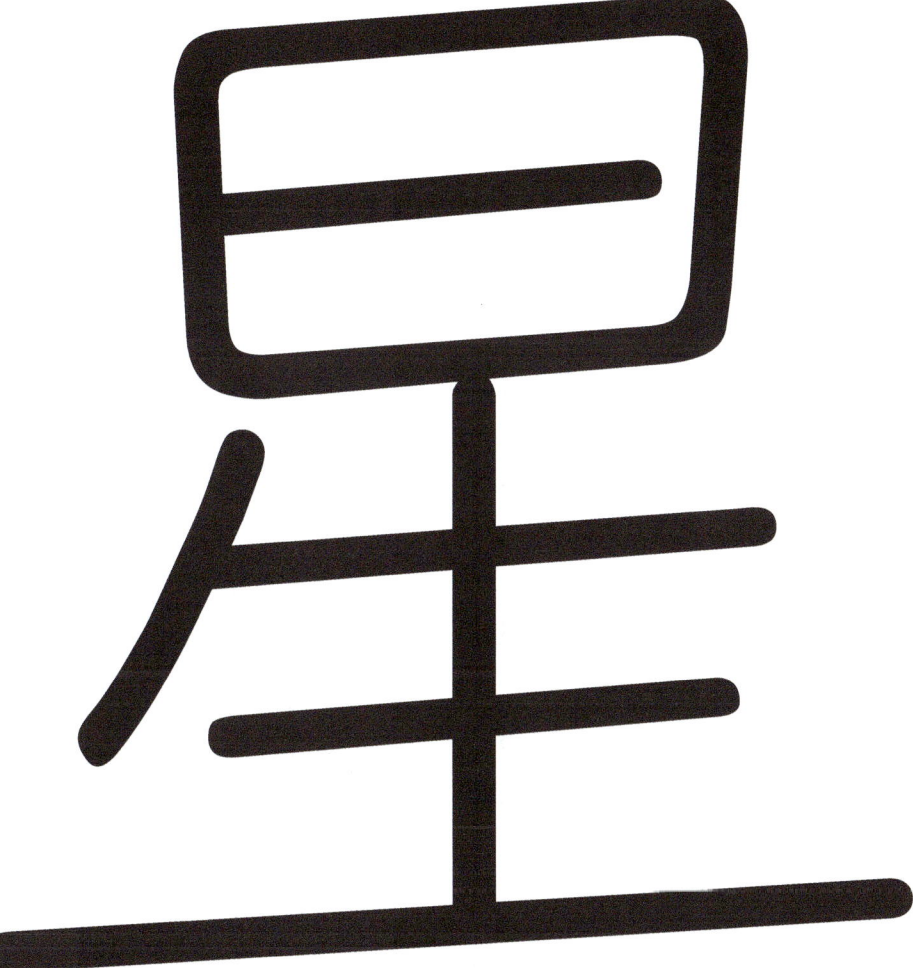

Describe your picture and write how you will remember what the character means and what it sounds like:

星

Simplified

XĪNG

star

星

Traditional

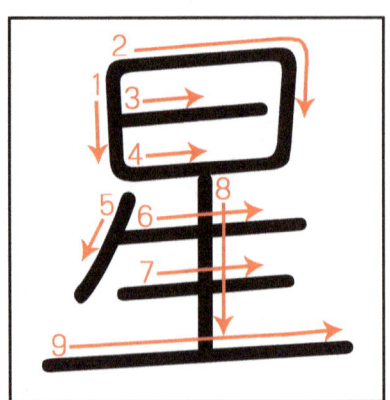

星期 XĪNGQĪ *week*

星星 XĪNGxing* *stars*

海星 hǎiXĪNG *sea star*

明星 mínGXĪNG *celebrity*

外星人 WàiXĪNGréN *space alien*

Strokes: 9

Radical: 日 Rì *'sun'*

Pinyin: xīng

Practice writing this character using the stroke order shown above.
When you're finished, circle the one that you like the best.

星 星 星 星 星 星

星 星 星 星 星 星 星

My Character Picture for
XĪNG *prosper*

Describe your picture and write how you will remember what the character means and what it sounds like:

名字＿＿＿＿＿＿＿＿＿＿＿＿＿＿＿＿＿ ＿＿＿年＿＿月＿＿日

 兴

Simplified

XĪNG

prosper

 興

Traditional

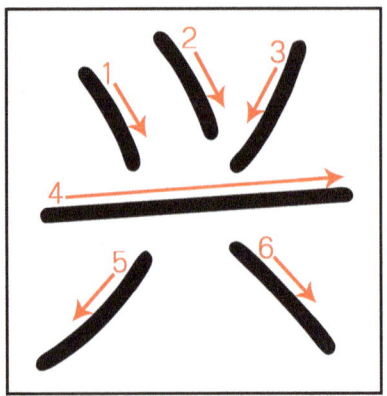

高兴 GĀOXĪNG *happy*

兴奋 XĪNGFèn *be excited*

兴趣 XìngQù *interest*

Strokes: 8

Radical: 八 BĀ '*eight*'

Pinyin: xīng

Practice writing this character using the stroke order shown above.
When you're finished, circle the one that you like the best.

My Character Picture for
Yào   *want/will*

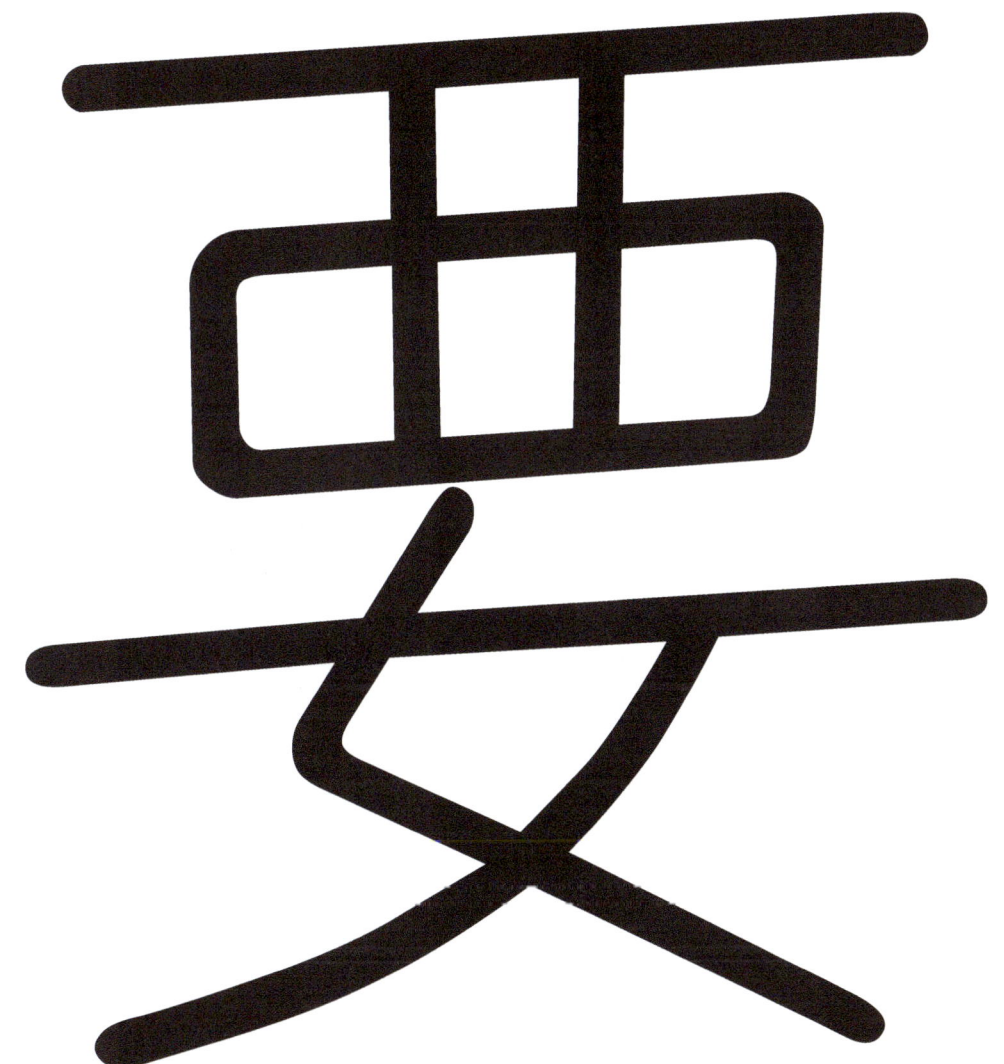

Describe your picture and write how you will remember what the character means and what it sounds like:

名字＿＿＿＿＿＿＿＿＿＿＿＿＿＿＿＿＿ ＿＿＿年 ＿＿月 ＿＿日

要
Simplified

Yào
want/will

要
Traditional

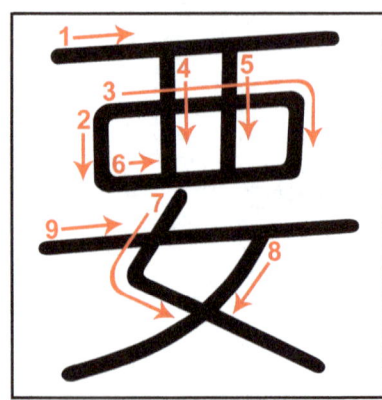

要 Yào *want*

不要 bÚYào *don't! don't want*

需要 XŪYào *need*

重要 ZhòngYào *important*

要求 YĀOqíU *demand*

Strokes: 9

Radical: 西 XĪ *'west'*

Pinyin: yào

Practice writing this character using the stroke order shown above.
When you're finished, circle the one that you like the best.

My Character Picture for
yě   *also/too*

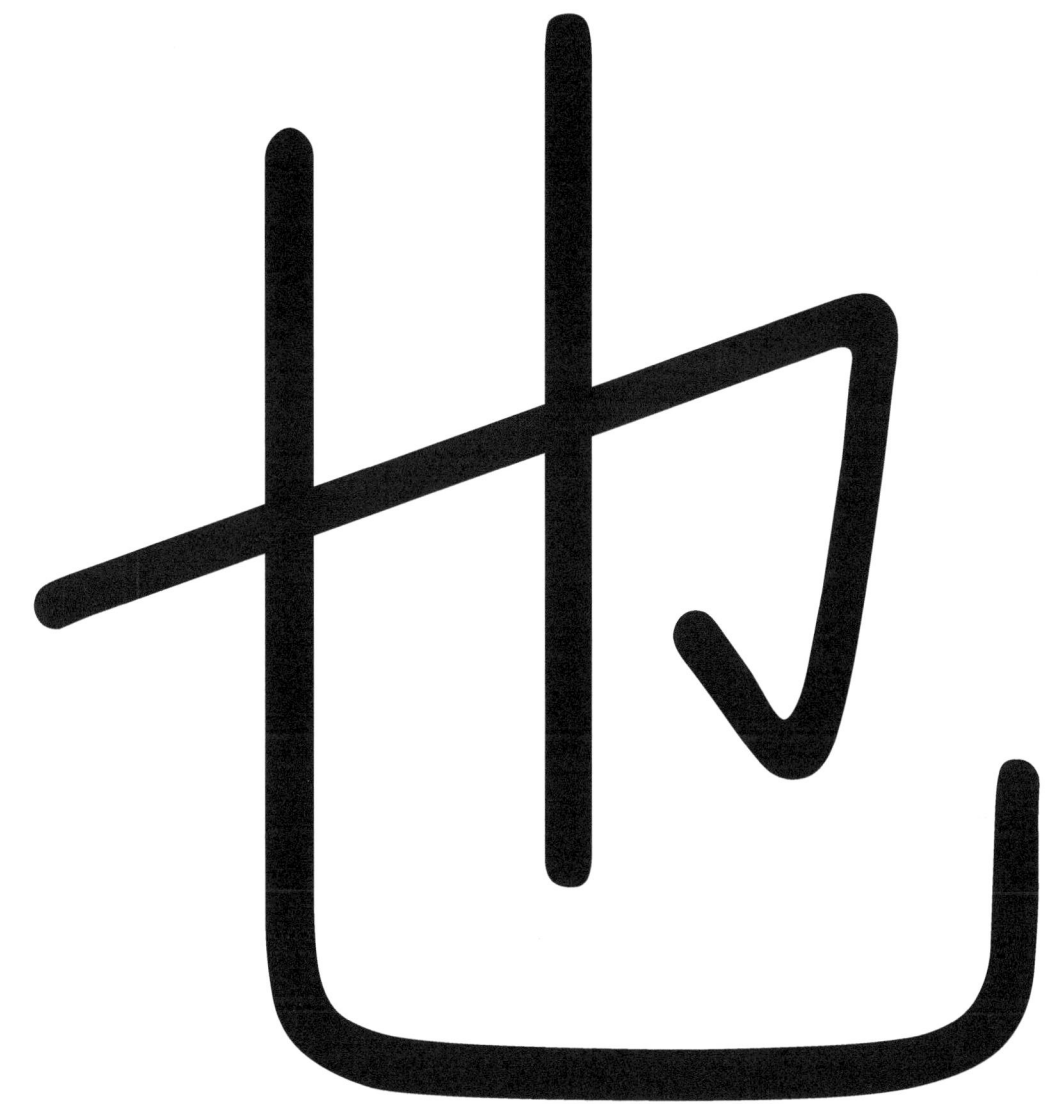

Describe your picture and write how you will remember what the character means and what it sounds like:

也
Simplified

yě
also / too

也
Traditional

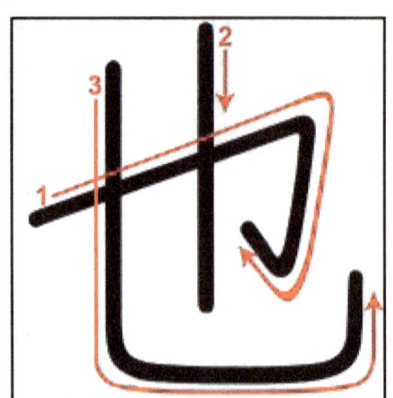

也　yě　*also*

也许　yěxǔ　*perhaps*

也好　yěhǎo　*may as well*

也是　yěShì　*be also the same*

也行　yěxínG　*All right!*

Strokes: 3

Radical: 乙 yǐ *'second'*

Pinyin: yě

Practice writing this character using the stroke order shown above.
When you're finished, circle the one that you like the best.

My Character Picture for
YĪ *clothes*

Describe your picture and write how you will remember what the character means and what it sounds like:

衣
Simplified

YĪ
clothes

衣
Traditional

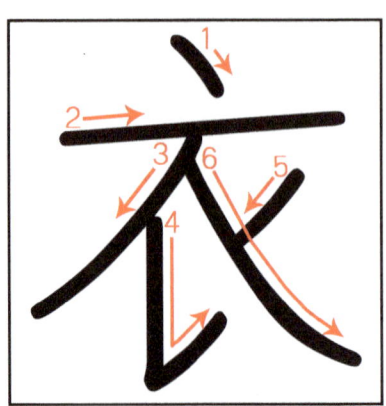

衣服 YĪfu* clothes

毛衣 máOYĪ sweater

雨衣 yǔYĪ raincoat

睡衣 ShuìYĪ pyjamas

内衣 NèiYĪ underwear

Strokes: 6

Radical: 衣 YĪ 'clothes'

Pinyin: yǐ

Practice writing this character using the stroke order shown above.
When you're finished, circle the one that you like the best.

衣 衣 衣 衣 衣 衣

衣 衣 衣 衣 衣 衣 衣

My Character Picture for

yǐ   *to use/so as to*

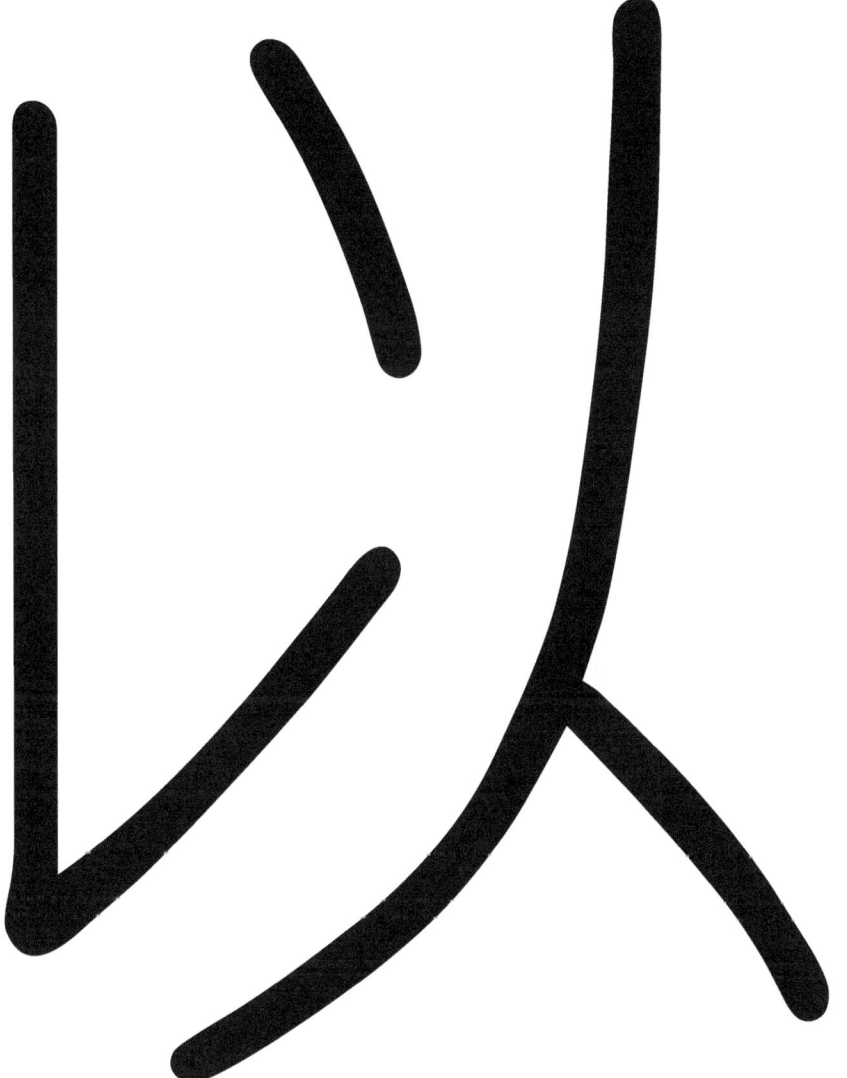

Describe your picture and write how you will remember what the character means and what it sounds like:

＿＿

＿＿

＿＿

以
Simplified

yǐ
to use / so as to

以
Traditional

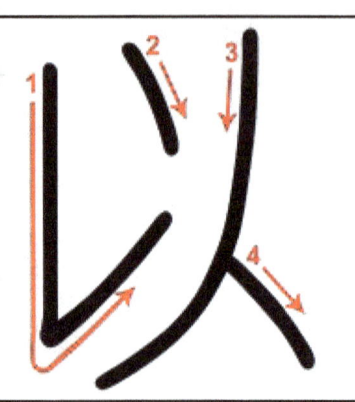

可以　kěyǐ　*allowed to*

以后　yǐHòu　*afterward*

所以　suǒyǐ　*therefore*

以前　yǐqiáN　*before*

以为　yǐWèi　*believe falsely*

Strokes: 4
Radical: 人 réN
　　　'person'
Pinyin: yǐ

Practice writing this character using the stroke order shown above.
When you're finished, circle the one that you like the best.

以

My Character Picture for
YĪN   *cause/reason/because*

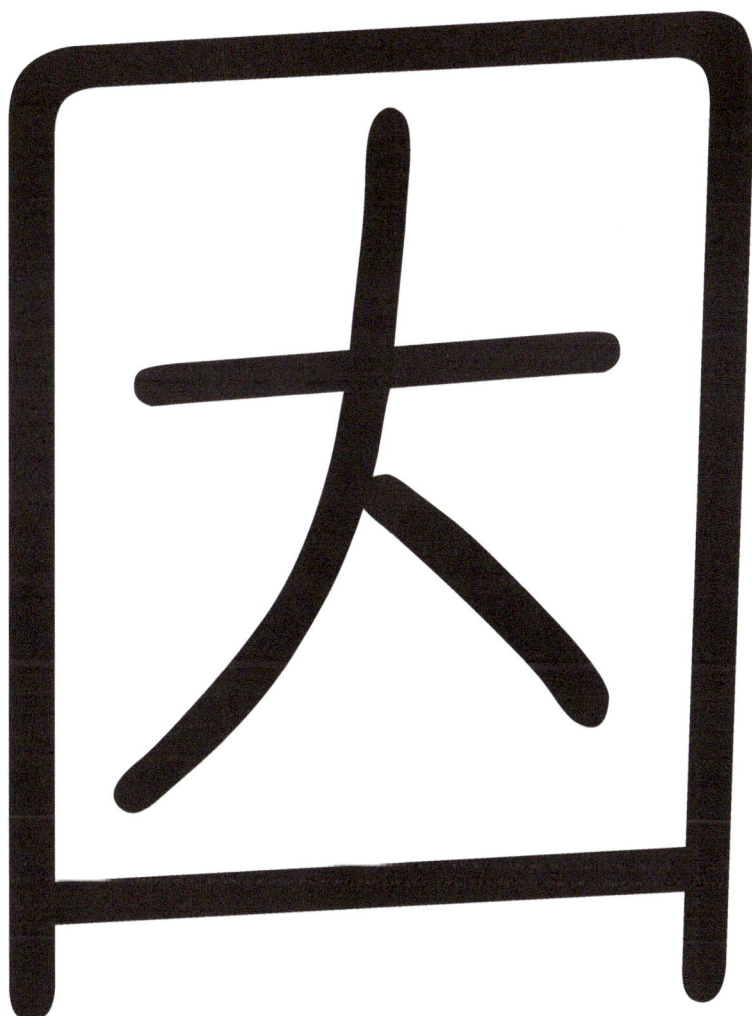

Describe your picture and write how you will remember what the character means and what it sounds like:

因
Simplified

YĪN
cause / reason / because

因
Traditional

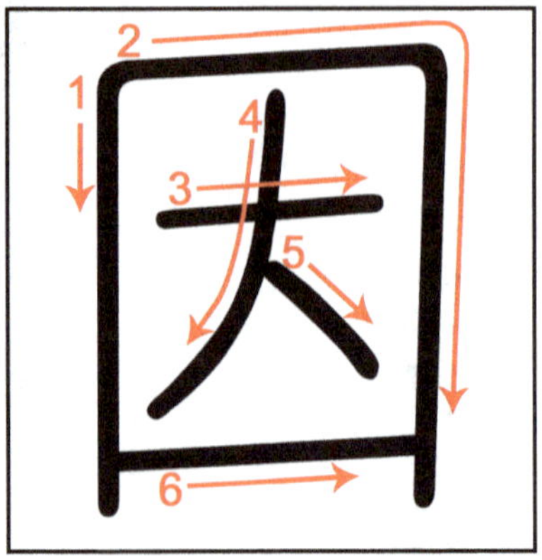

因为 YĪNWèi *because*

因此 YĪNcǐ *therefore*

原因 yuáNYĪN *cause, reason*

因而 YĪN'éR *consequently*

Strokes: 6

Radical: 囗 wéI
'enclosure'

Pinyin: yīn

Practice writing this character using the stroke order shown above.
When you're finished, circle the one that you like the best.

My Character Picture for
YĪNG   *hero/excellent*

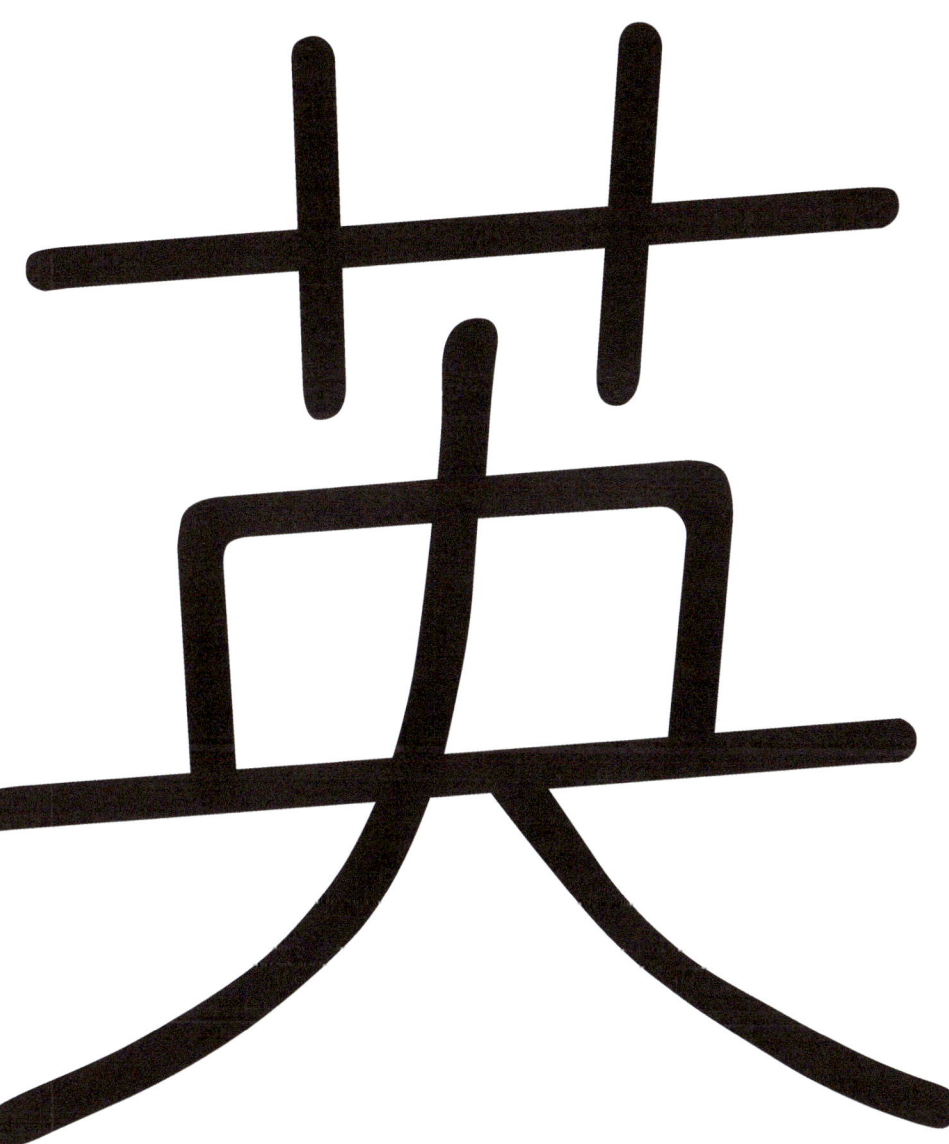

Describe your picture and write how you will remember what the character means and what it sounds like:

英
Simplified

YĪNG

hero/excellent

英
Traditional

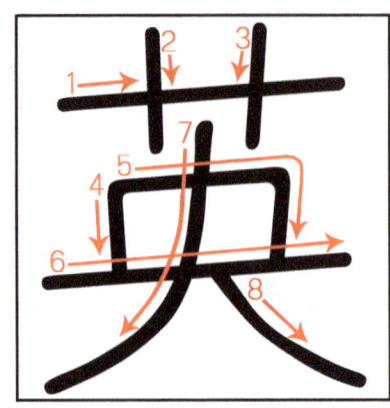

英国 YĪNGguÓ *England*

英语 YĪNGyǔ *English (language)*

英雄 YĪNGxiónG *hero*

英明 YĪNGmínG *brilliance*

英里 YĪNGlǐ *mile*

Strokes: 8

Radical: 艹 (艸) cǎo 'grass'

Pinyin: yīn

Practice writing this character using the stroke order shown above. When you're finished, circle the one that you like the best.

My Character Picture for
yǐng   *shadow*

Describe your picture and write how you will remember what the character means and what it sounds like:

影

yǐng
shadow

影 Simplified   影 Traditional

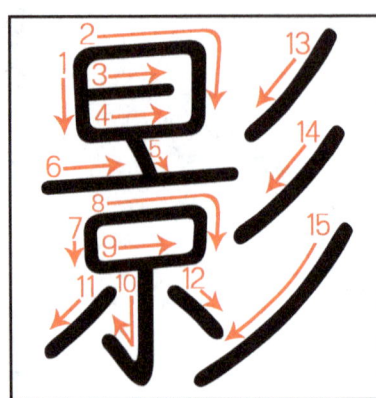

电影 Diànyǐng *movie*

影星 yǐngXĪNG *movie star*

电影院 DiànyǐngYuàn
movie theater

影子 yǐngzi* *shadow*

Strokes: 15

Radical: 彡 SHĀN
'bristle'

Pinyin: yǐng

Practice writing this character using the stroke order shown above.
When you're finished, circle the one that you like the best.

影

My Character Picture for
yǒu   to have/there is

Describe your picture and write how you will remember what the character means and what it sounds like:

有 yǒu

Simplified 有

Traditional 有

to have / there is

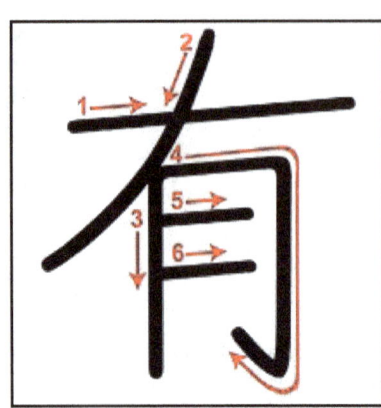

有 yǒu   *have, there is*

没有 méIyǒu   *don't have, there isn't*

有的 yǒude*   *some*

有些 yǒuXIĒ   *there are a few*

只有 zhǐyǒu   *there are only*

Strokes: 6

Radical: 月 Yuè 'moon'

Pinyin: yǒu

Practice writing this character using the stroke order shown above.
When you're finished, circle the one that you like the best.

有　有　有　有　有　有

有　有　有　有　有　有　有

My Character Picture for
yǒu   *friend*

Describe your picture and write how you will remember what the character means and what it sounds like:

友

Simplified

yǒu

friend

友

Traditional

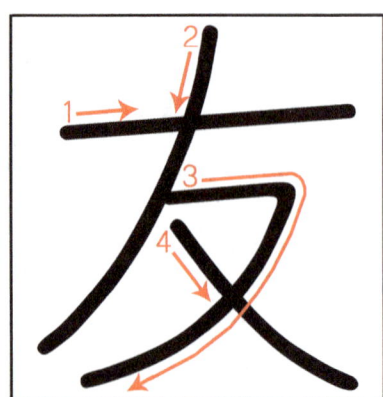

朋友 pénGyou* *friend*

小朋友 xiǎopénGyou* *children*

男朋友 náNpénGyou* *boyfriend*

女朋友 nǚpénGyou* *girlfriend*

友好 yǒuhǎo *friendship/close friend*

Strokes: 4

Radical: 又 Yòu
'again'

Pinyin: yǒu

*Practice writing this character using the stroke order shown above.
When you're finished, circle the one that you like the best.*

友　友　友　友　友　友

友　友　友　友　友　友　友

180

My Character Picture for

yǔ *language*

Describe your picture and write how you will remember what the character means and what it sounds like:

语

yǔ
language

語

Simplified

Traditional

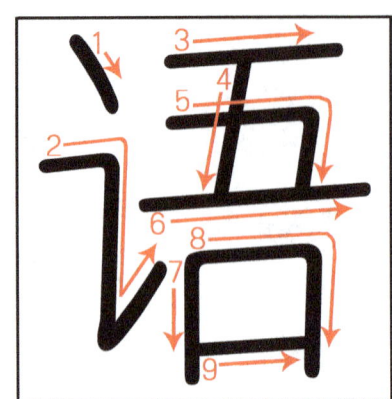

语言 yǔyáN *language*

英语 YĪNGyǔ *English language*

汉语 Hànyǔ *Chinese language (used in China)*

国语 guÓyǔ *Chinese language (used in Taiwan)*

语法 yǔfǎ *grammar*

Strokes: 9

Radical: 讠(言) yáN 'speech'

Pinyin: yǔ

Practice writing this character using the stroke order shown above. When you're finished, circle the one that you like the best.

语 语 语 语 语 语

語 语 语 语 语 语 语 语

My Character Picture for

Yuè *moon, month*

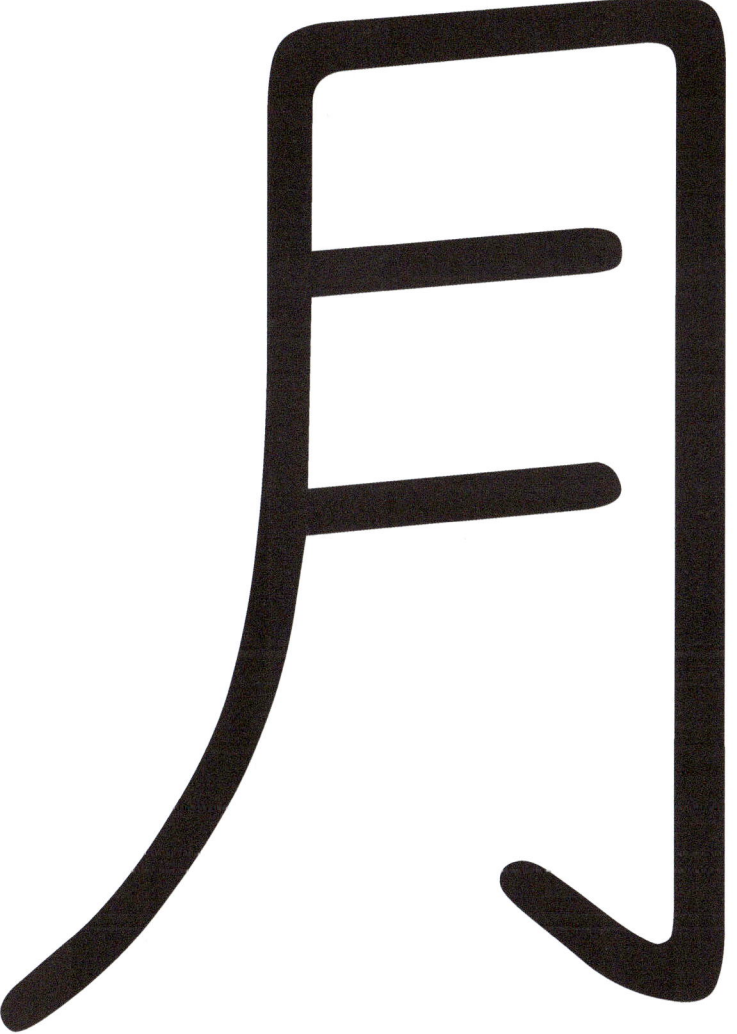

Describe your picture and write how you will remember what the character means and what it sounds like:

月
Simplified

Yuè
moon, month

月
Traditional

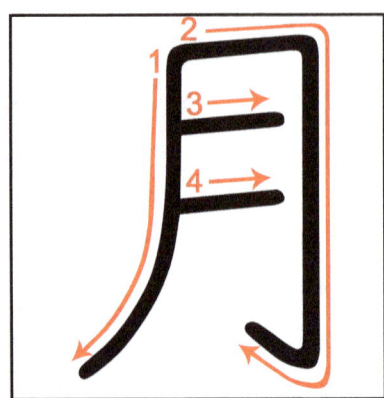

月 Yuè *moon, month*

十月 shíYuè *October*

月亮 Yuèliang* *moon*

月光 YuèGUĀNG *moonlight, moonbeam*

月球 YuèqíU *The Moon*

Strokes:

Radical: 月 Yuè *'moon'*

Pinyin: yuè

Practice writing this character using the stroke order shown above.
When you're finished, circle the one that you like the best.

月 月 月 月 月 月

My Character Picture for

Zài   be at, in or on (a place)

Describe your picture and write how you will remember what the character means and what it sounds like:

Zài

be at, in, or on (a place)

在 Simplified

在 Traditional

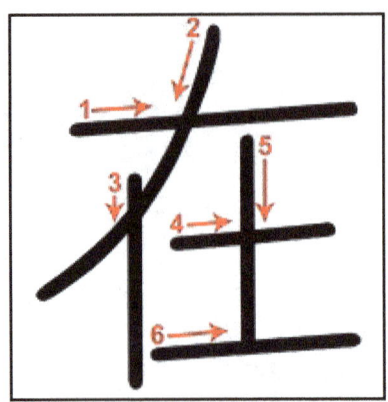

在　Zài　*be at, in, or on (a place)*

现在　XiànZài　*now*

正在　ZhèngZài　*in the process of*

在家　ZàiJIĀ　*be at home*

在线　ZàiXiàn　*be online*

Strokes: 6

Radical: 土 tǔ *'earth'*

Pinyin: zài

Practice writing this character using the stroke order shown above.
When you're finished, circle the one that you like the best.

在

在 在 在 在 在

拃 在 在 在 在 在 在 在

My Character Picture for
zěn *how*

Describe your picture and write how you will remember what the character means and what it sounds like:

名字________________________ ________年 ______月 ______日

怎 zěn 怎

Simplified — how — Traditional

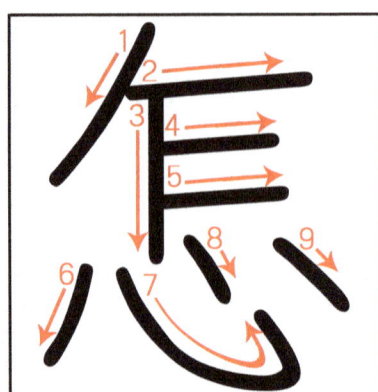

怎 zěn *how, why*

怎么 zěnme* *how*

怎么样 zěnme*Yàng *how are things?*

怎么办 zěnme*Bàn *what's to be done?*

怎样 zěnYàng *how?*

Strokes: 9

Radical: 心 XĪN *'heart'*

Pinyin: zěn

Practice writing this character using the stroke order shown above. When you're finished, circle the one that you like the best.

怎	怎	怎	怎	怎	怎

怎 怎 怎 怎 怎 怎 怎 怎 怎

My Character Picture for
Zhè   *this/these*

Describe your picture and write how you will remember what the character means and what it sounds like:

这
Simplified

Zhè
this / these

這
Traditional

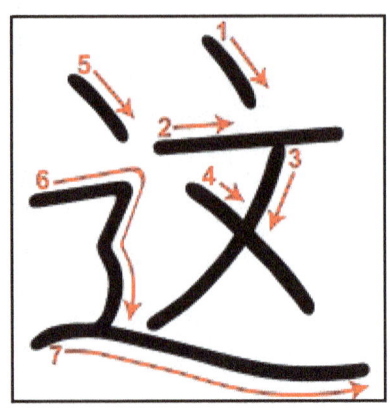

这样 ZhèYàng *this way*

这个 Zhège* *this one*

这些 ZhèXIĒ *these*

这么 Zhème* *so; such*

这里 Zhèlǐ *here*

Strokes: 7

Radical: 辶 CHUŌ
'*walking*'

Pinyin: zhè / zhèi

Practice writing this character using the stroke order shown above.
When you're finished, circle the one that you like the best.

这 这 这 这 这 这

这 这 这 这 这 这 这 这

My Character Picture for

zhǐ, ZHĪ   *only, measure word for certain animals*

Describe your picture and write how you will remember what the character means and what it sounds like:

只
Simplified

zhǐ, ZHĪ

only /
measure word for certain animals

只
Traditional

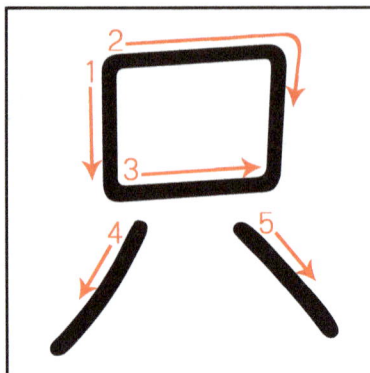

只 zhǐ *only*

一只猫 YĪZHĪMĀO *a cat*

只要 zhǐYào *so long as*

只有 zhǐyǒu *only, alone*

只是 zhǐShì *merely, just*

Strokes: 5

Radical: 口 kǒu
'mouth'

Pinyin: zhī, zhǐ

*Practice writing this character using the stroke order shown above.
When you're finished, circle the one that you like the best.*

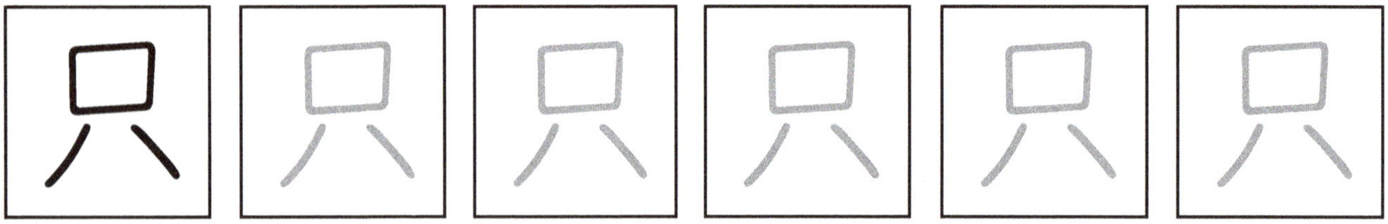

名字＿＿＿＿＿＿＿＿＿＿＿＿＿＿＿＿＿＿＿＿ ＿＿＿年 ＿＿月 ＿＿日

My Character Picture for
ZHĪ *know*

Describe your picture and write how you will remember what the character means and what it sounds like:

ZHĪ

know

知
Simplified

知
Traditional

知道 ZHĪDào *knows*

不知道 BùZHĪDào *don't know*

知识 ZHĪshi* *knowledge*

知名 ZHĪmínG *famous*

Strokes: 8

Radical: 矢 shí
'*arrow*'

Pinyin: zhī

*Practice writing this character using the stroke order shown above.
When you're finished, circle the one that you like the best.*

知　知　知　知　知　知

My Character Picture for
ZHŌNG   *middle/in*

Describe your picture and write how you will remember what the character means and what it sounds like:

Simplified

ZHŌNG

middle / in

Traditional

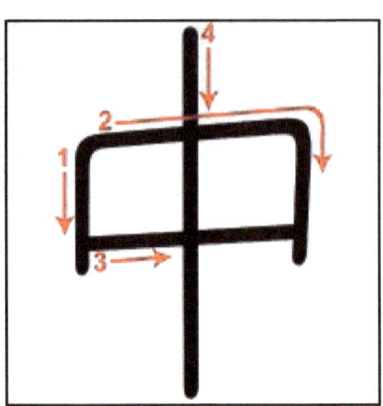

中国 ZHŌNGguÓ *China*

中心 ZHŌNGXĪN *center*

中间 ZHŌNGJIĀN *in between*

中央 ZHŌNGwéN *Chinese language*

中学 ZHŌNGxuÉ *middle school*

Strokes: 4

Radical: 丨 gǔn
'*vertical stroke*'

Pinyin: zhōng / zhòng

Practice writing this character using the stroke order shown above.
When you're finished, circle the one that you like the best.

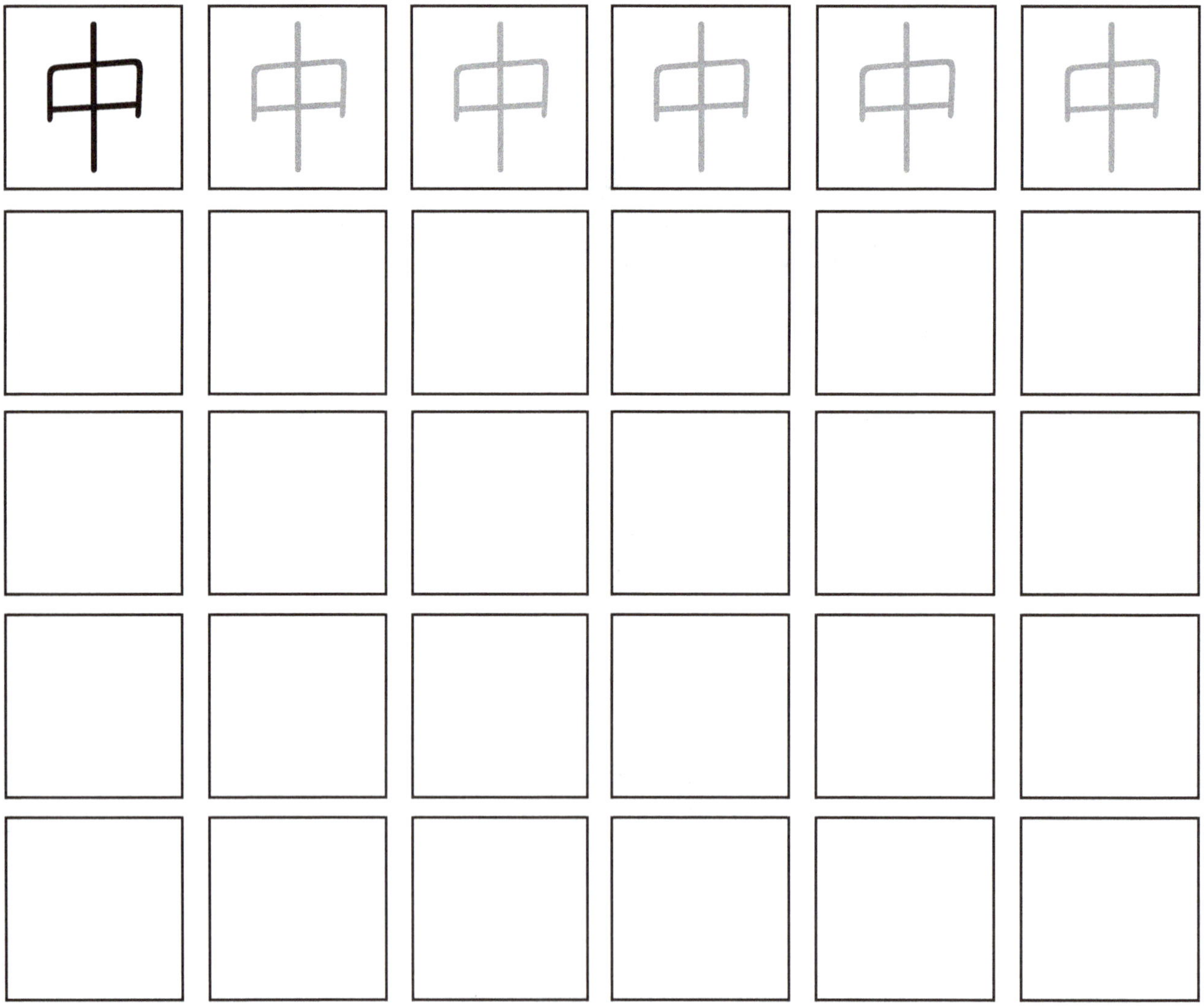

My Character Picture for
ZHŌNG   *clock/bell*

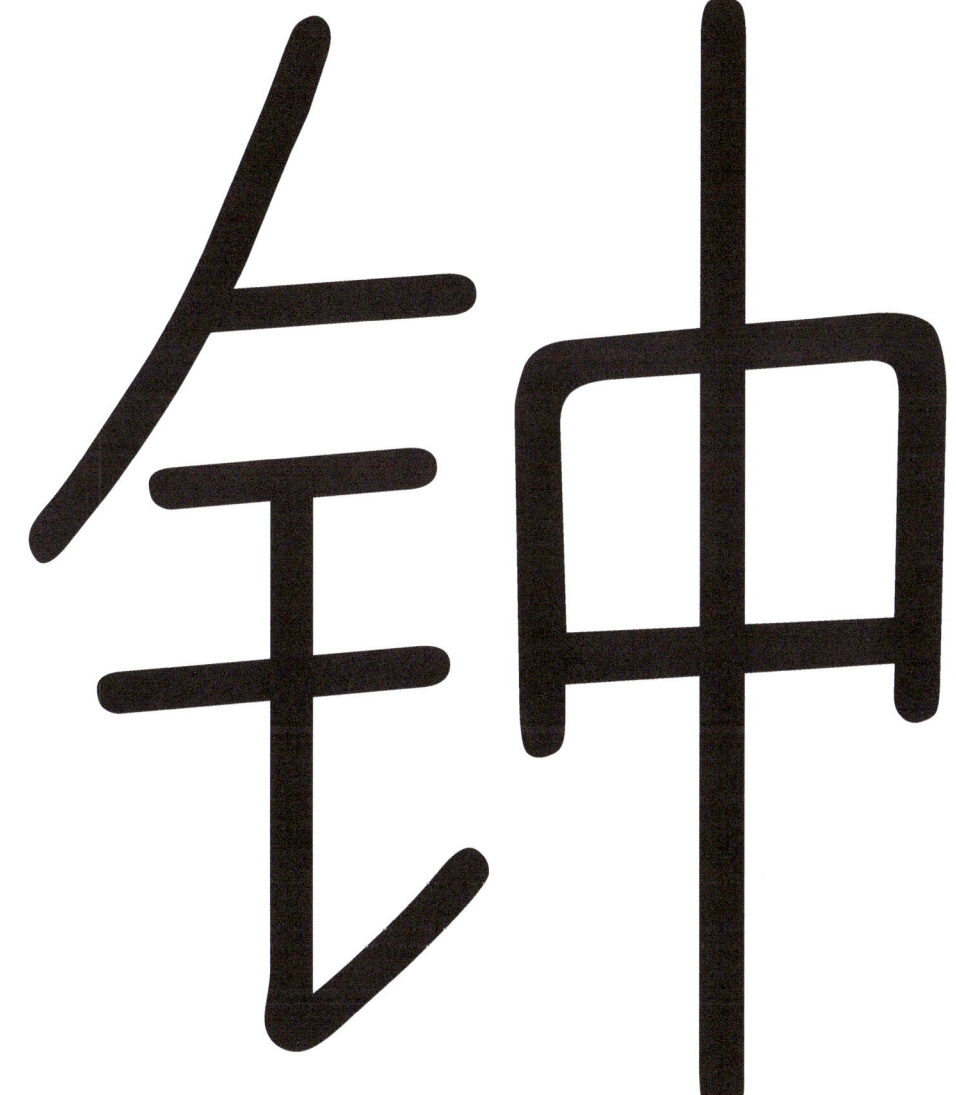

Describe your picture and write how you will remember what the character means and what it sounds like:

钟 ZHŌNG 鐘

Simplified

clock / bell

Traditional

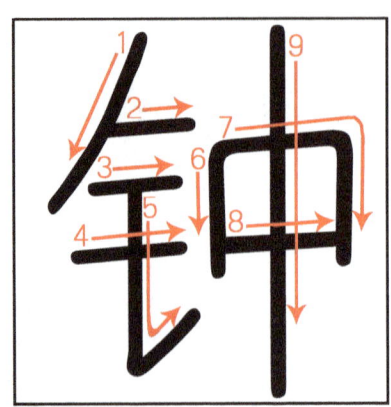

钟头　ZHŌNGtóU　*hour*

分钟　FĒNZHŌNG　*minute*

秒钟　miǎoZHŌNG　*second*

一分钟　YĪFĒNZHŌNG　*one minute*

点钟　diǎnZHŌNG　*o'clock*

Strokes: 9

Radical: 钅(金) JĪN
'*gold*'

Pinyin: zhōng

*Practice writing this character using the stroke order shown above.
When you're finished, circle the one that you like the best.*

钟　钟　钟　钟　钟　钟

鐘　钟　钟　钟　钟　钟　钟　钟　钟

My Character Picture for
zi* *(noun suffix)*

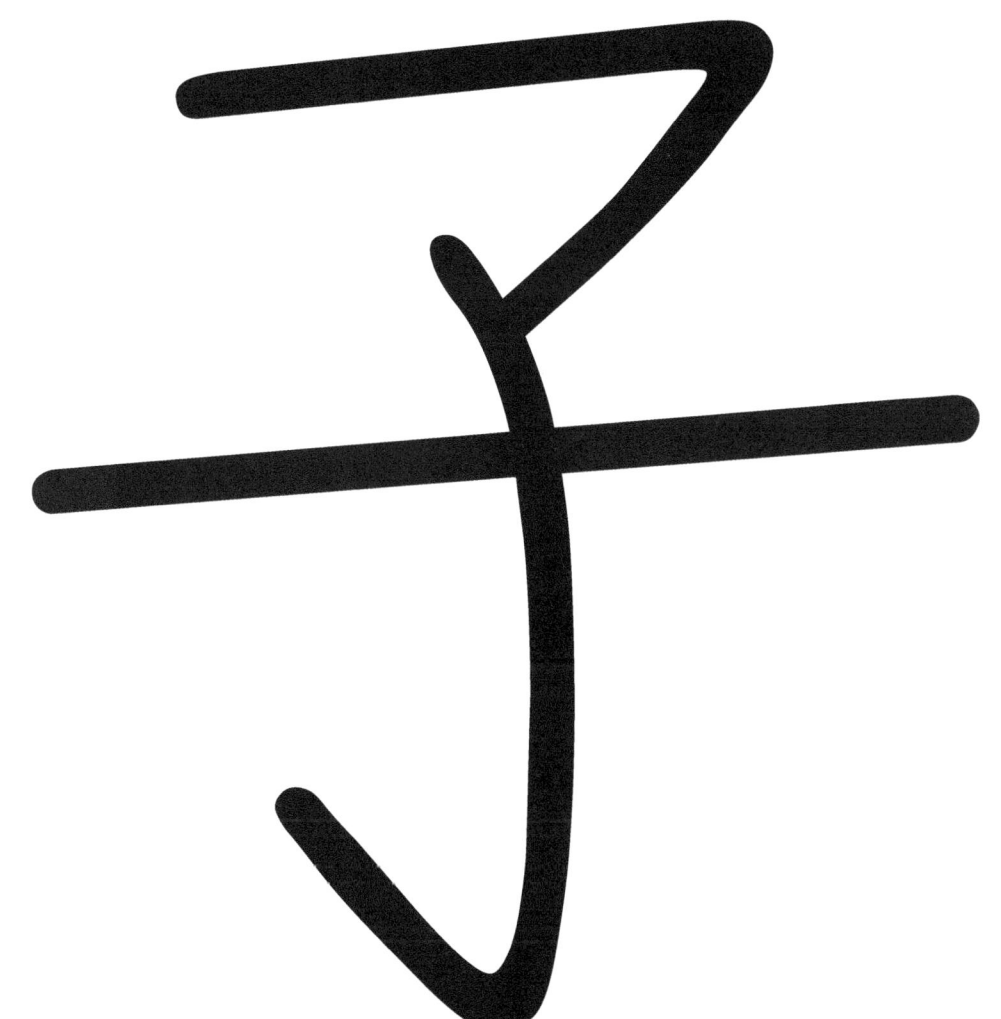

Describe your picture and write how you will remember what the character means and what it sounds like:

名字_____   _____年 _____月 _____日

Simplified

zi*

(noun suffix)

Traditional

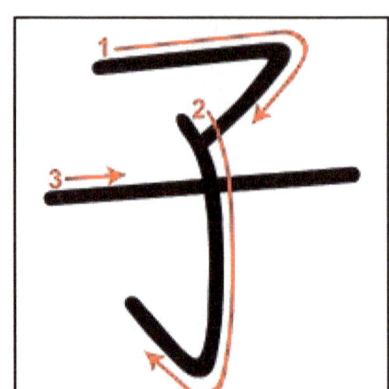

孩子 háIzi*   *child*

包子 BĀOzi*   *steamed stuffed bun*

饺子 jiǎozi*   *dumpling*

房子 fánGzi*   *house*

儿子 éRzi*   *son*

Strokes: 3

Radical: 子 zǐ 'son'

Pinyin: zǐ / zi

Practice writing this character using the stroke order shown above.
When you're finished, circle the one that you like the best.

子   子   子   子   子   子

子 子 子 子 子 子 子 子 子

200

名字________________________________ ________年 _____月 _____日

My Character Picture for

YĪ *one*

一

My Character Picture for

Èr *two*

二

My Character Picture for

SĀN *three*

三

My Character Picture for

Sì *four*

四

My Character Picture for

wǔ *five*

五

名字＿＿＿＿＿＿＿＿＿＿＿＿＿＿＿＿＿＿ ＿＿＿＿年 ＿＿＿月 ＿＿＿日

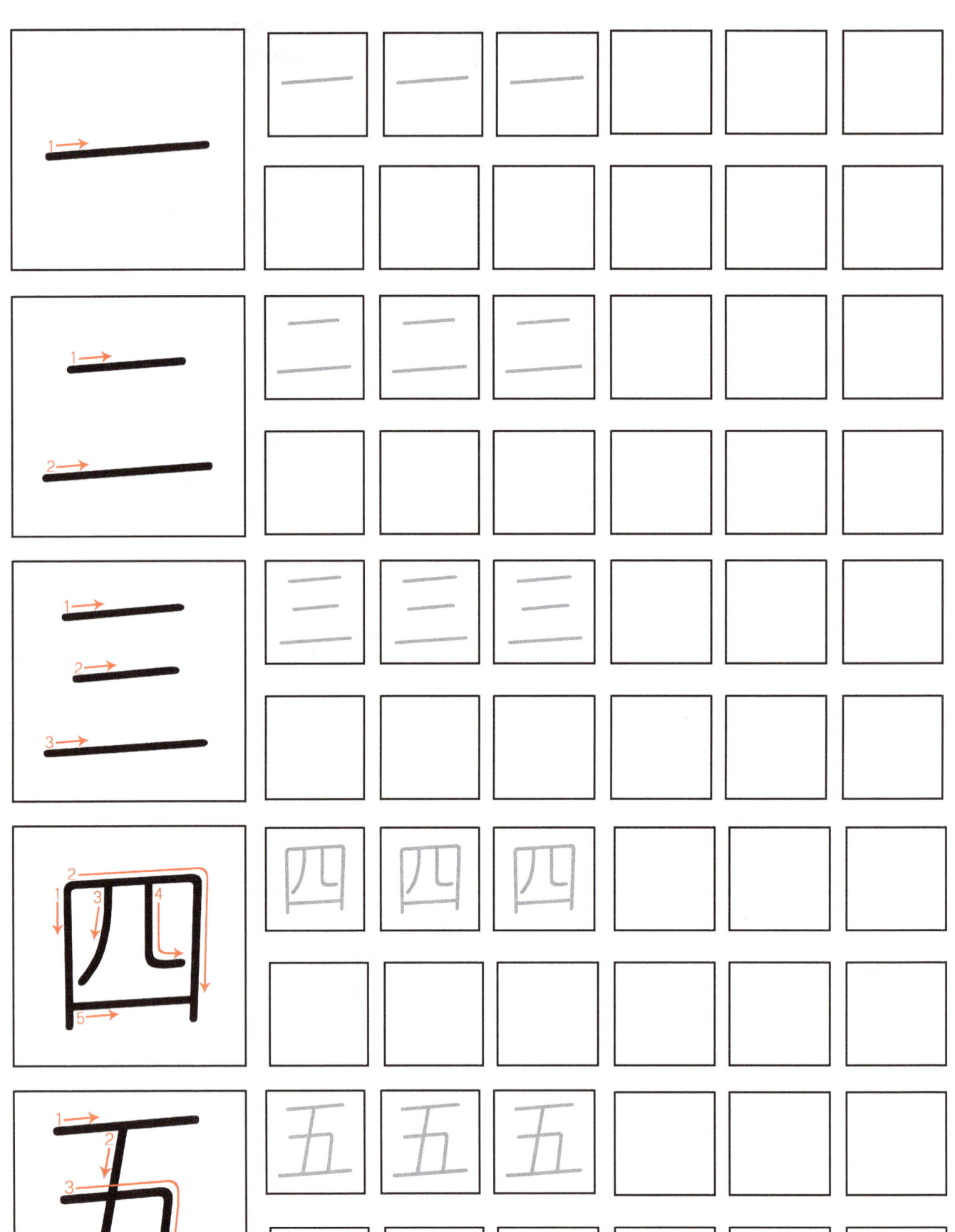

My Character Picture for
Liù *six*

My Character Picture for
QĪ *seven*

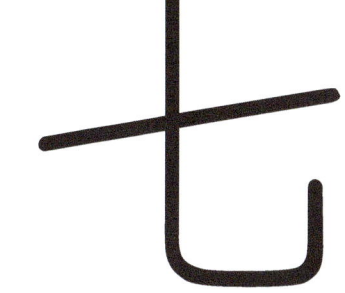

My Character Picture for
BĀ *eight*

My Character Picture for
jiǔ *nine*

My Character Picture for
shí *ten*

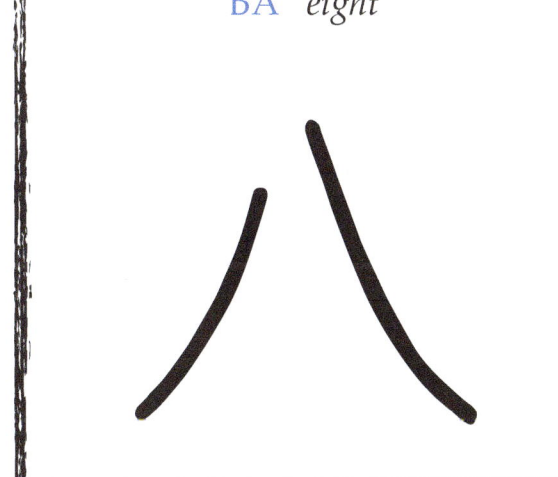

My Character Pictures for

My Character Picture for
bǎi *hundred*

百

My Character Picture for
QIĀN *thousand*

千

My Character Picture for
Wàn *ten thousand*

万

My Character Picture for
Yì *hundred million*

亿

名字________________________ ________年 _____月 _____日

My Character Pictures for

hónGSè *red*

红色

chénGSè *orange*

橙色

huánGSè *yellow*

黃色

Practice writing these characters using the stroke orders shown.
When you're finished, circle the ones that you like the best.

red

hónG   Sè

orange

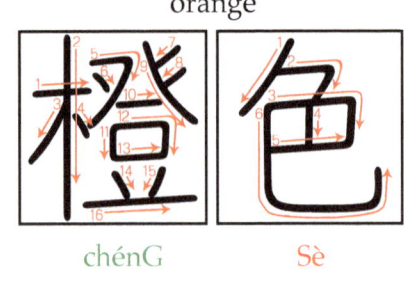
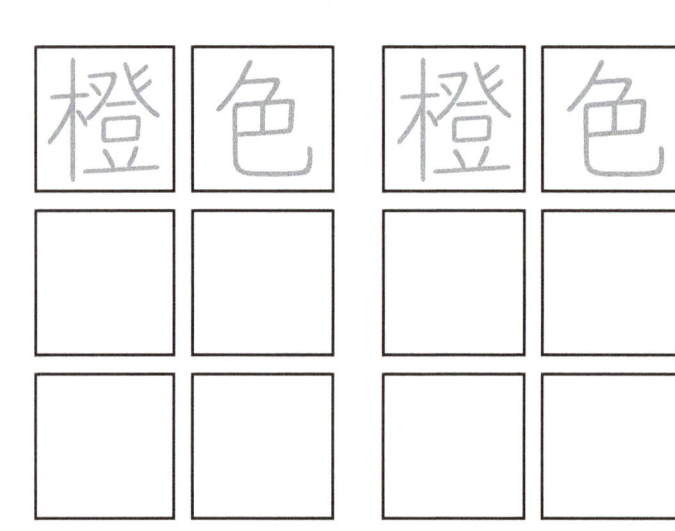

chénG   Sè

yellow

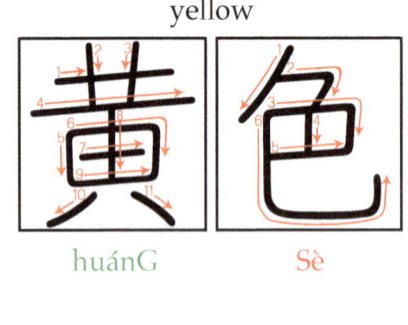
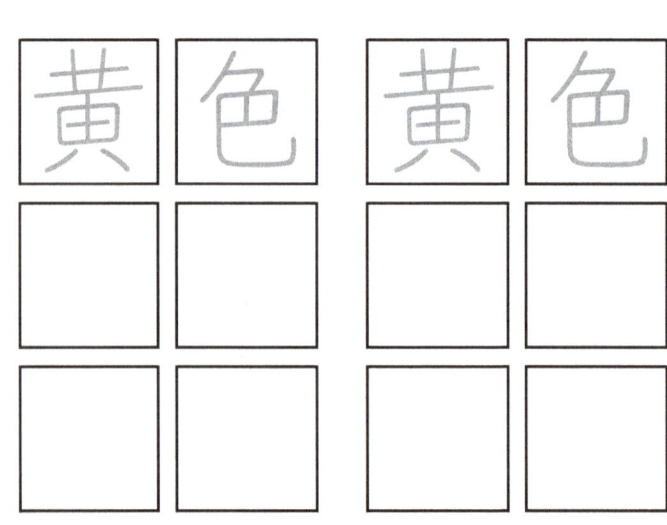

huánG   Sè

名字________________ ______年 _____月 _____日

My Character Pictures for

LǜSè *green*

绿色

lánSè *blue*

蓝色

zǐSè *purple*

紫色

Practice writing these characters using the stroke orders shown.
When you're finished, circle the ones that you like the best.

green

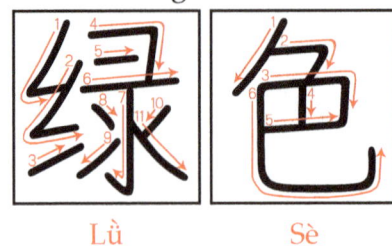

Lǜ   Sè

blue

lán   Sè

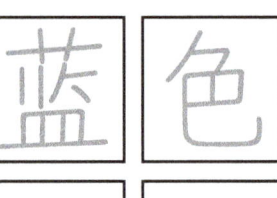 

 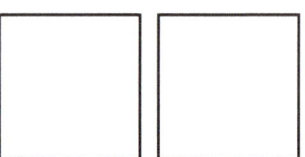

purple

zǐ   Sè

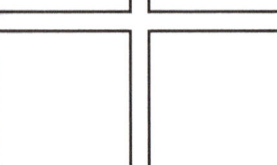 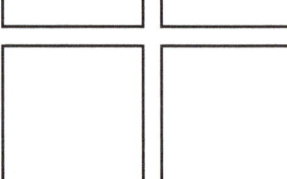

名字________________ ______年 ____月 ____日

My Character Pictures for

HUĪSè *gray*

灰色

báISè *white*

白色

HĒISè *black*

黑色

Practice writing these characters using the stroke orders shown.
When you're finished, circle the ones that you like the best.

gray

white

black

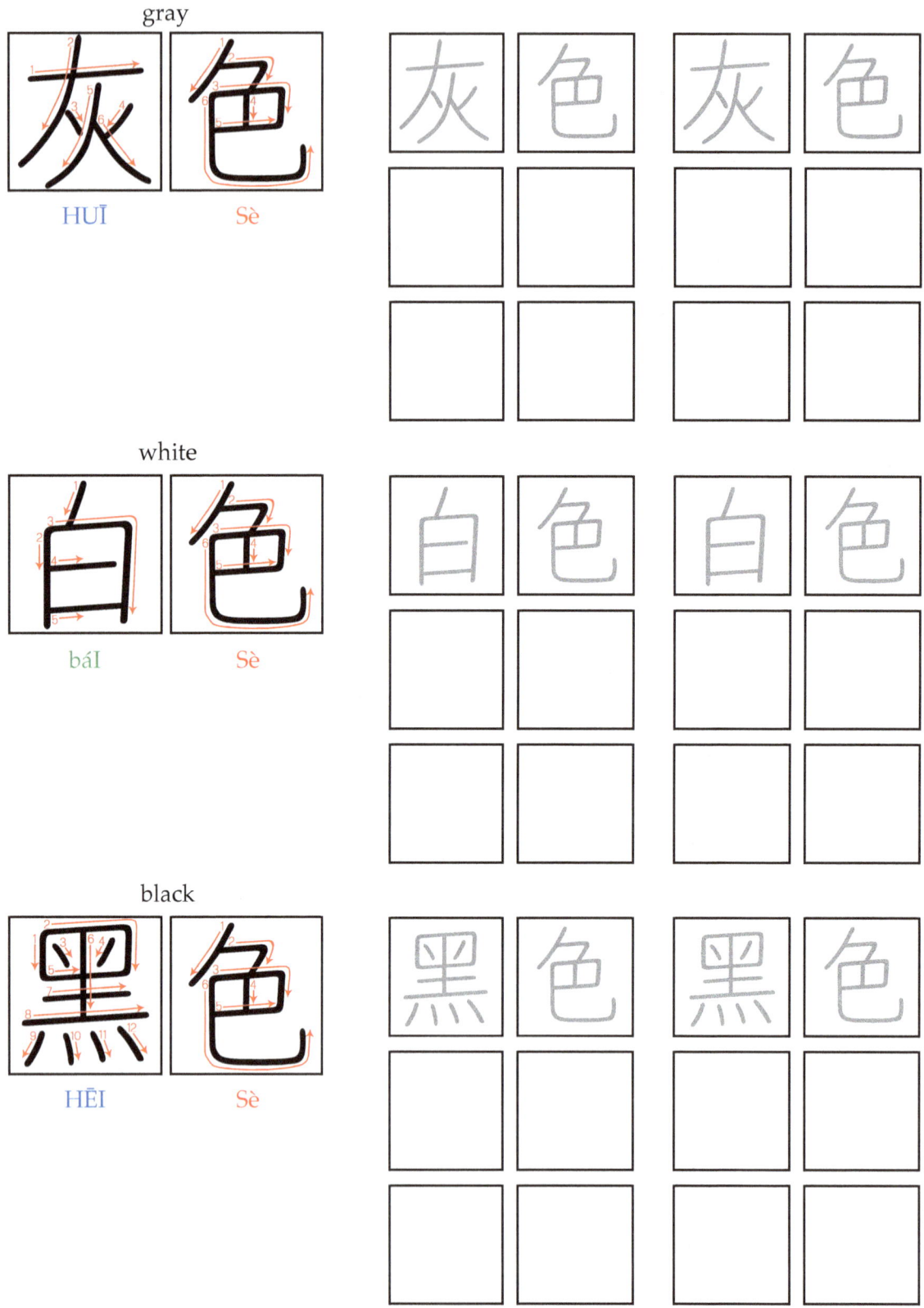

HUĪ   Sè

báI   Sè

HĒI   Sè

My Character Pictures for

fěnhónGSè *pink*

KĀFĒISè *brown*

Practice writing these characters using the stroke orders shown.
When you're finished, circle the ones that you like the best.

pink

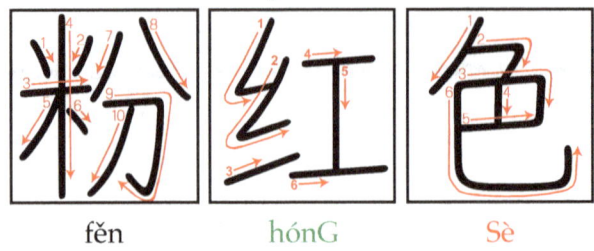

fěn hónG Sè

brown

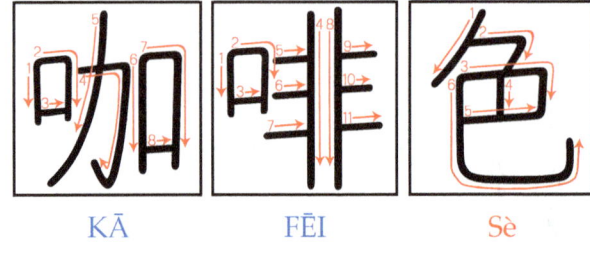

KĀ FĒI Sè

My Character Pictures for

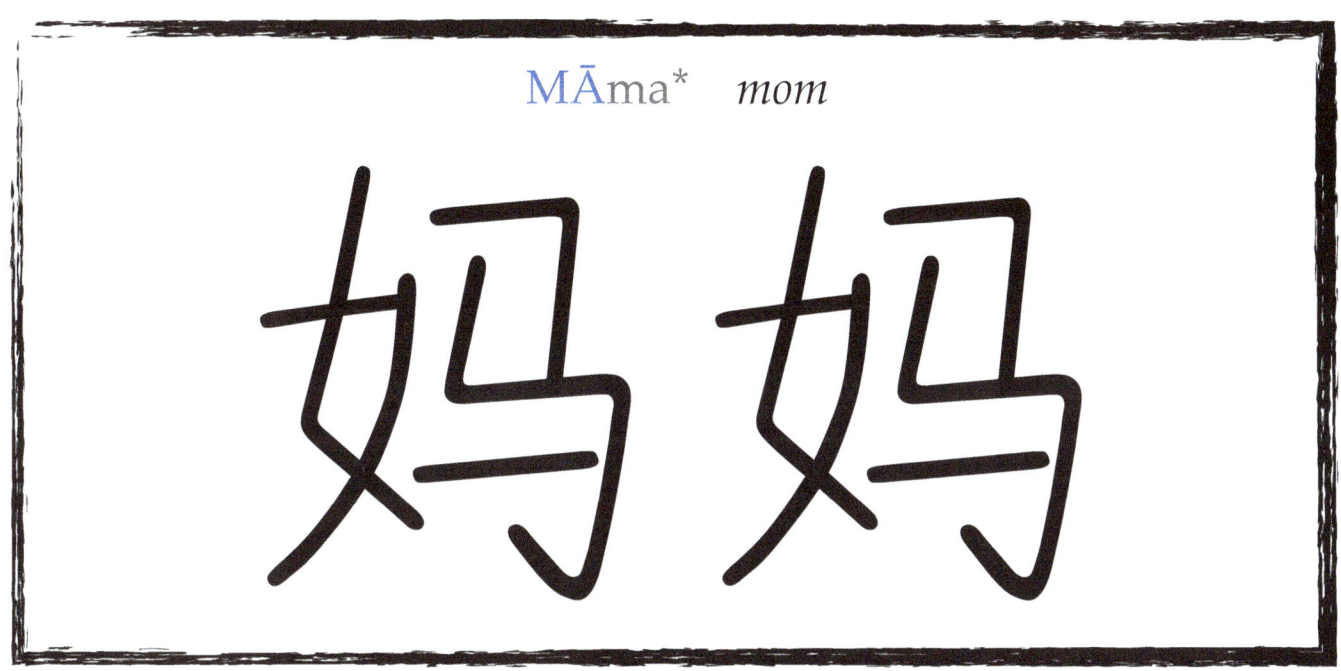

MĀma* *mom*

Bàba* *dad*

Practice writing these characters using the stroke orders shown.
When you're finished, circle the ones that you like the best.

mom

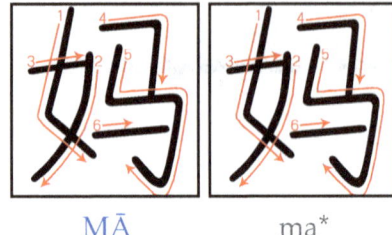

MĀ ma*

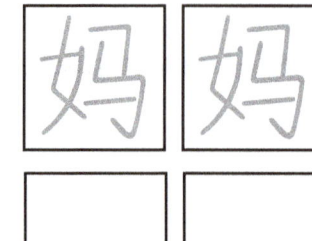

dad

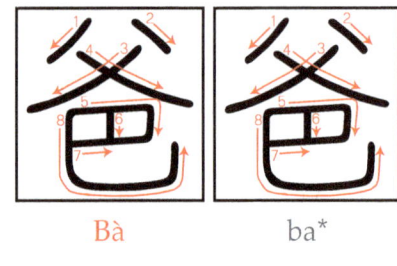

Bà ba*

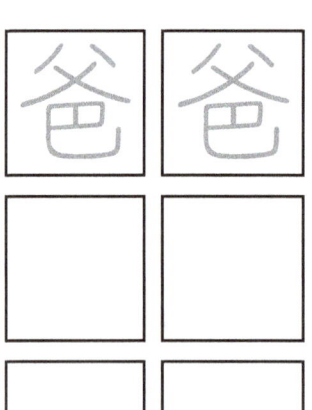

My Character Pictures for

*jiĕ*jie*   *older sister*

姐姐

*GĒ*ge*   *older brother*

哥哥

Practice writing these characters using the stroke orders shown.
When you're finished, circle the ones that you like the best.

older sister

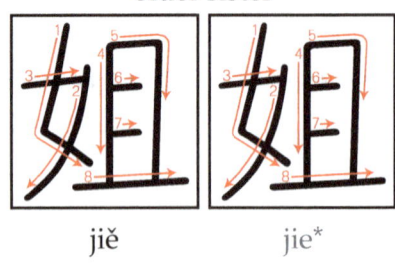

jiě   jie*

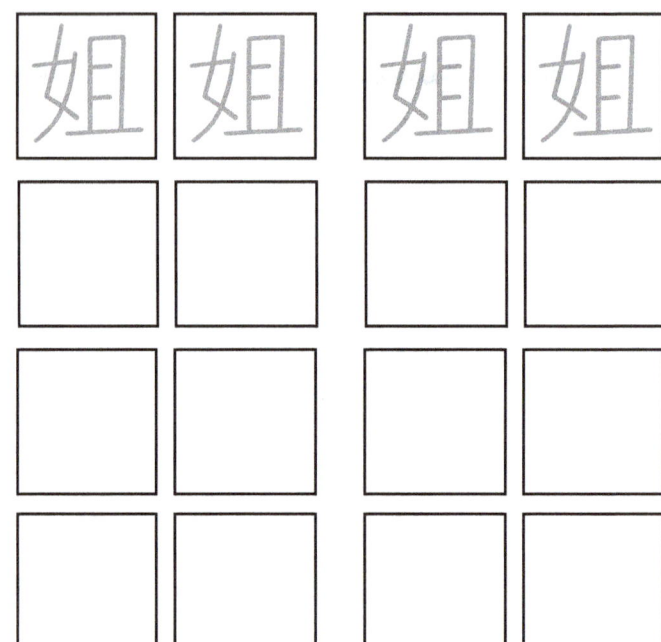

older brother

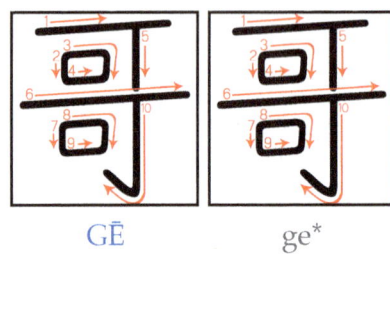

GĒ   ge*

名字______________________ ______年 ____月 ____日

My Character Pictures for

Mèimei* *younger sister*

妹妹

Dìdi* *younger brother*

弟弟

Practice writing these characters using the stroke orders shown.
When you're finished, circle the ones that you like the best.

younger sister

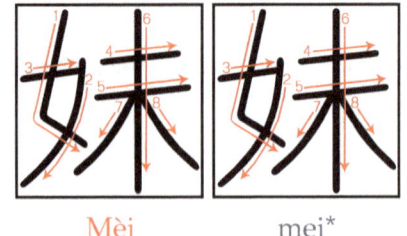

Mèi　　　mei*

younger brother

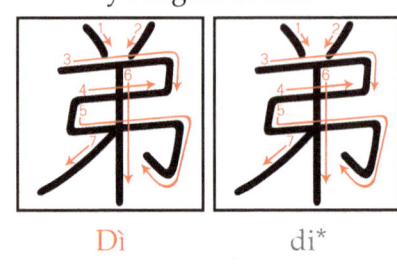

Dì　　　di*

My Character Pictures for

*năi*nai*   *grandma*

奶 奶

yÉye   *grandpa*

爷 爷

Practice writing these characters using the stroke orders shown.
When you're finished, circle the ones that you like the best.

grandma

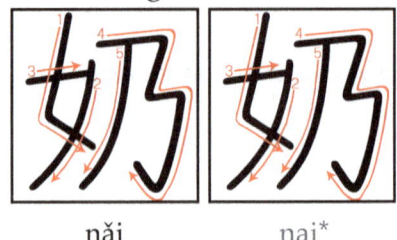

nǎi   nai*

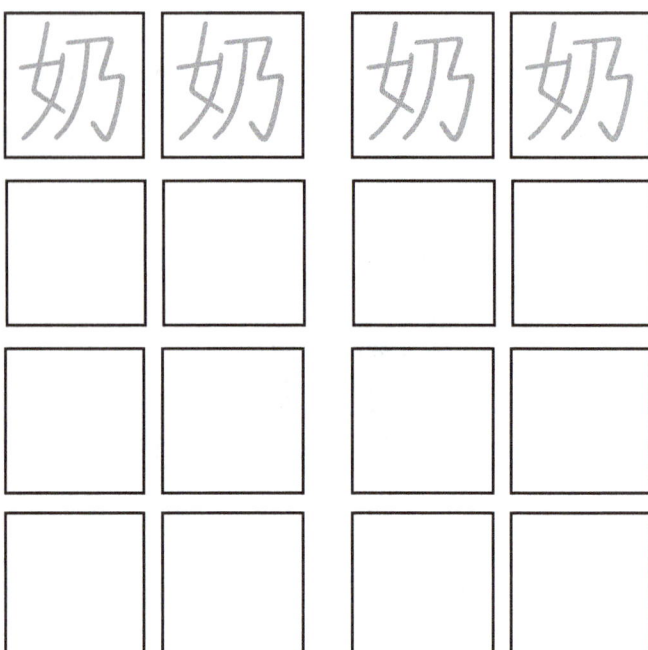

grandpa

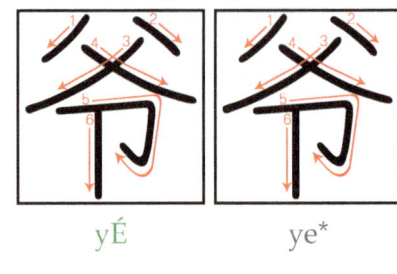

yÉ   ye*

名字________________________________ ________年 _____月 _____日

PĪSà *pizza*

披萨

tăKĒ *taco*

塔科

HànbăoBĀO *hamburger*

汉堡包

Practice writing these characters using the stroke orders shown.
When you're finished, circle the ones that you like the best.

pizza

PĪ　　　Sà

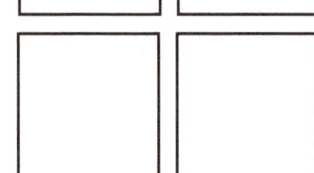

taco

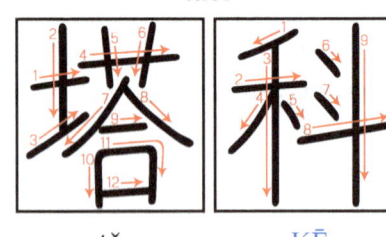 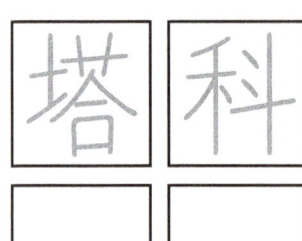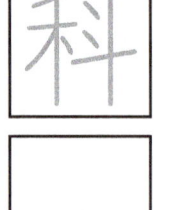

tǎ　　　KĒ

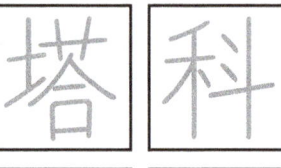

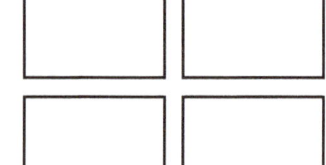

hamburger

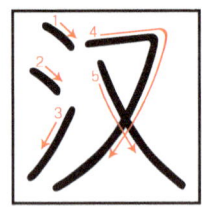 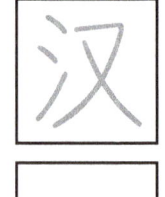

Hàn　　bǎo　　BĀO

My Character Pictures for

Règǒu   *hot dog*

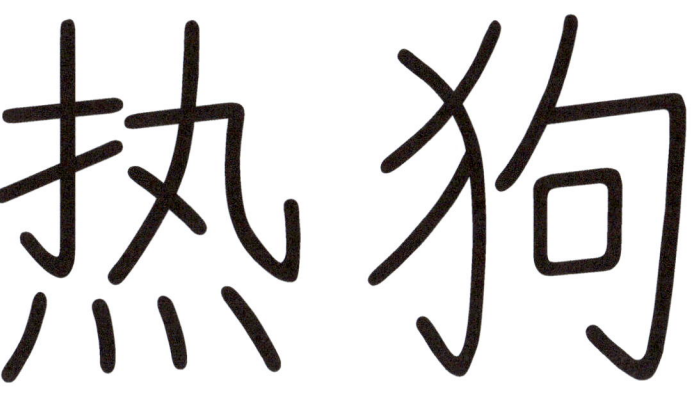

热狗

SHĀLĀ   *salad*

沙拉

SĀNmínGZhì   *sandwich*

三明治

225

Practice writing these characters using the stroke orders shown.
When you're finished, circle the ones that you like the best.

hot dog

Rè　　　gǒu

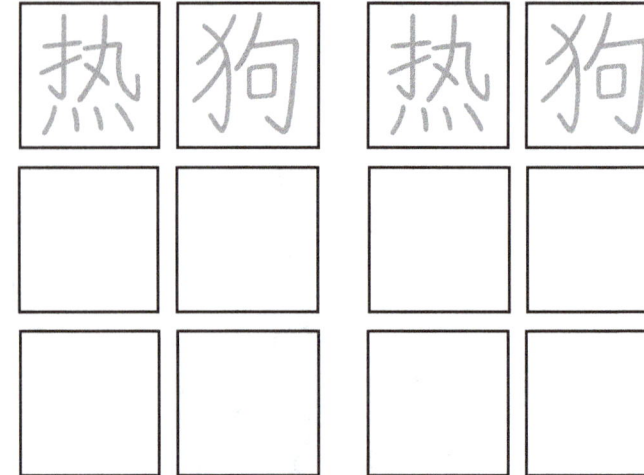

salad

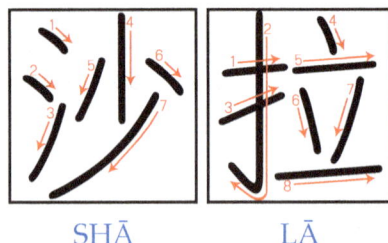

SHĀ　　　LĀ

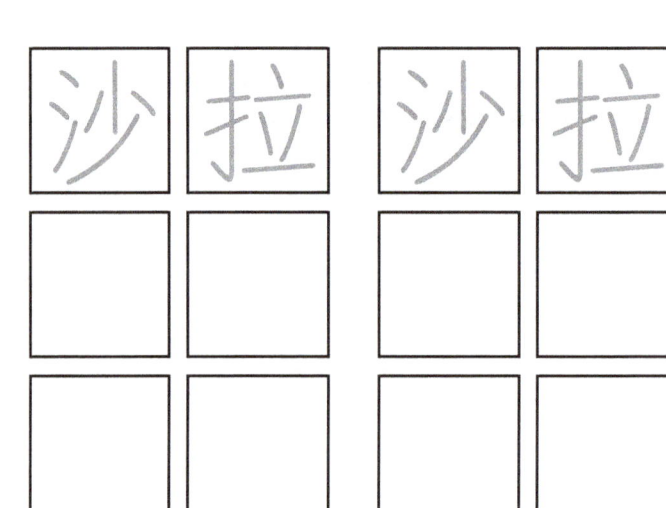

sandwich

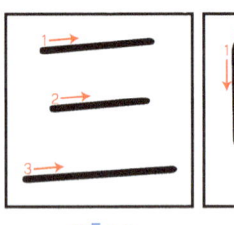 

SĀN　　mínG　　Zhì

My Character Pictures for

mǐ**Fàn**   *rice (cooked)*

MiàntiáO   *noodles*

shuǐjiǎo   *dumplings*

水饺

Practice writing these characters using the stroke orders shown.
When you're finished, circle the ones that you like the best.

rice (cooked)

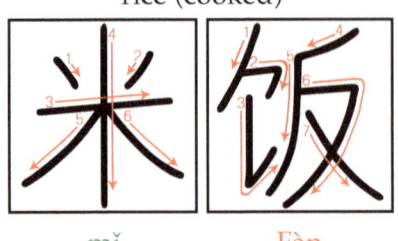

mǐ   Fàn

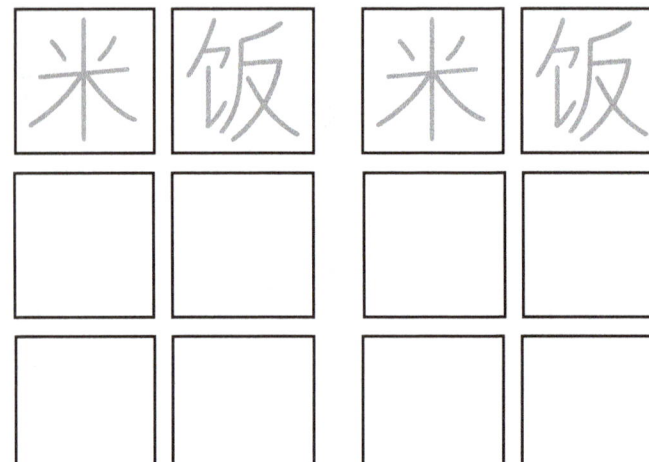

noodles

Miàn   tiáO

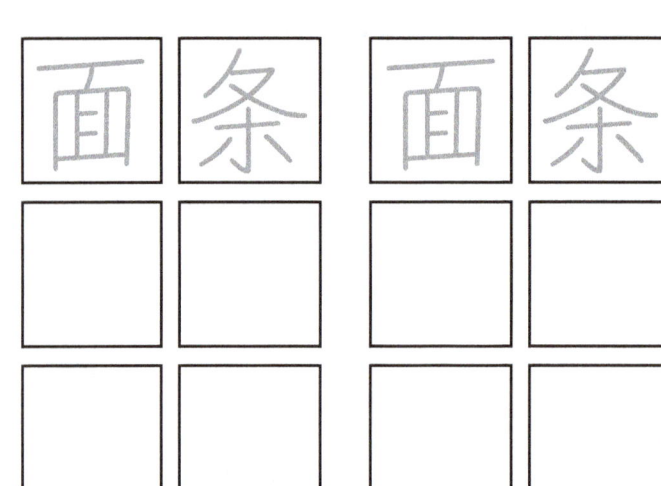

dumplings

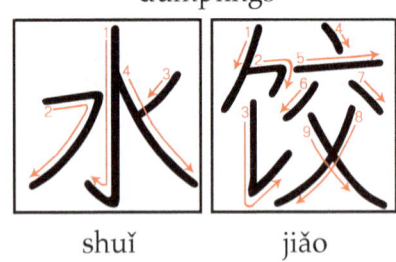

shuǐ   jiǎo

228

My Character Pictures for

niÚRòu   *beef*

牛 肉

ZHŪRòu   *pork*

猪 肉

JĪRòu   *chicken (meat)*

鸡 肉

Practice writing these characters using the stroke orders shown.
When you're finished, circle the ones that you like the best.

beef

niÚ　Ròu

pork

ZHŪ　Ròu

chicken

JĪ　Ròu

名字________________________　________年 ______月 ______日

My Character Pictures for

Dòufu* *tofu*

豆腐

qiǎoKèLì *chocolate*

巧克力

BĪNGqÍlíN *ice cream*

冰淇淋

Practice writing these characters using the stroke orders shown.
When you're finished, circle the ones that you like the best.

tofu

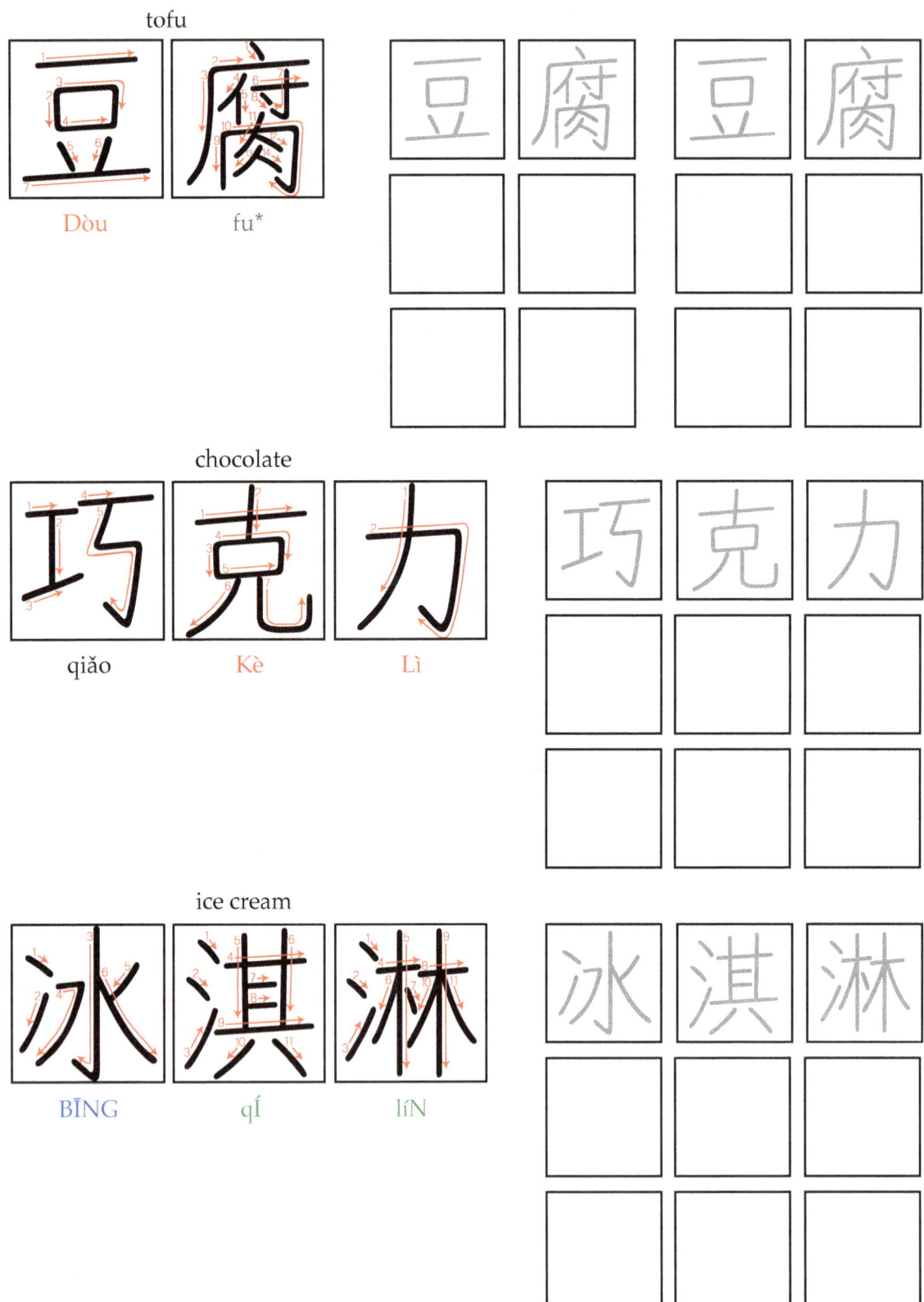

Dòu   fu*

chocolate

qiǎo   Kè   Lì

ice cream

BĪNG   qÍ   líN

My Character Pictures for

pínGguǒ   *apple*

XIĀNGJIĀO   *banana*

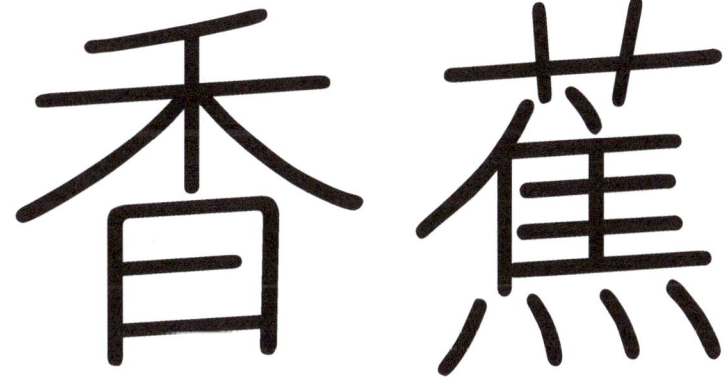

cǎoméI   *strawberry*

草莓

Practice writing these characters using the stroke orders shown.
When you're finished, circle the ones that you like the best.

apple

pínG guǒ

banana

XIĀNG JIĀO

strawberry

cǎo méI

My Character Pictures for

táOzi* *peach*

桃 子

chénGzi* *orange*

橙 子

XĪGUĀ *watermelon*

西 瓜

Practice writing these characters using the stroke orders shown.
When you're finished, circle the ones that you like the best.

peach

桃 táO
子 zi*

orange

橙 chénG
子 zi*

watermelon

西 XĪ
瓜 GUĀ

名字______________________________ ________年 _____月 _____日

My Character Pictures for

chÁ *tea*

茶

tánG *soup*

汤

niÚnǎi *milk*

牛奶

kěLè *cola*

可乐

Practice writing these characters using the stroke orders shown.
When you're finished, circle the ones that you like the best.

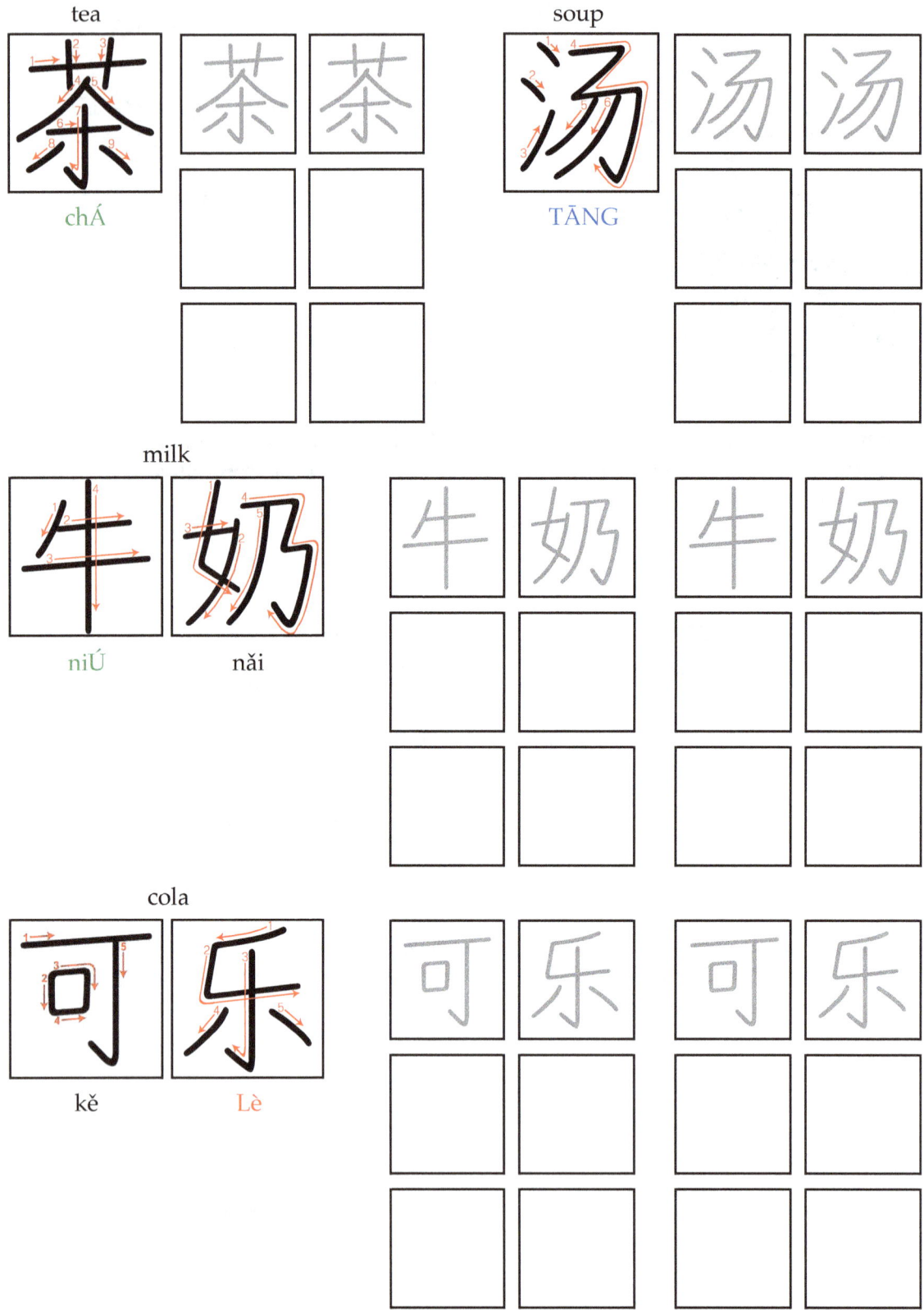

tea

茶

chÁ

soup

汤

TĀNG

milk

牛 奶

niÚ nǎi

cola

可 乐

kě Lè

Index

ENGLISH	PĪNYĪN	汉字	pages
after that, and then	ráNHòu	然后	109, 43
afterward	yǐHòu	以后	169, 43
also	yě	也	165
although	SUĪráN	虽然	133, 109
am / is / are	Shì	是	127
America	měiguÓ	美国	79, 29
and	hÉ	和	39
apple	pínGguǒ	苹果	233
banana	XIĀNGJIĀO	香蕉	233
because	YĪNWèi	因为	171, 149
beef	niÚRòu	牛肉	229
birthday	SHĒNGRì	生日	123, 113
black	HĒISè	黑色	211
blue	lánSè	蓝色	209
book	SHŪ	书	129
brother (older)	GĒge*	哥哥	217
brother (younger)	Dìdi*	弟弟	219
brown	KĀFĒISè	咖啡色	213
but, yet	DànShì	但是	5, 127
buys	mǎi	买	71
can, may	kěyǐ	可以	59, 169
chicken (meat)	JĪRòu	鸡肉	229
China	ZHŌNGguÓ	中国	195, 29
Chinese (language)	Hànyǔ	汉语	33, 181
Chinese (language)	ZHŌNGwéN	中文	195, 151
chocolate	qiǎoKèLì	巧克力	231

ENGLISH	PĪNYĪN	汉字	pages
clothes	Yīfu*	衣服	167, 21
cola	kěLè	可乐	237
comes	láI	来	65
cool, is cool	Kù	酷	63
country	guÓJIĀ	国家	29, 51
cries	KŪ	哭	61
Dad	Bàba*	爸爸	215
doesn't have	méIyǒu	没有	77, 177
doesn't want	bÚYào	不要	1, 163
dumplings	shuǐjiǎo	水饺	227
eats	CHĪ	吃	3
English (language)	YĪNGwéN	英文	173, 151
family / home	JIĀ	家	51
feels like eating	xiǎngCHĪ	想吃	157, 3
friend	pénGyou*	朋友	99, 179
goes	Qù	去	107
good, is good	hǎo	好	35
grandma	nǎinai*	奶奶	221
grandpa	yÉye*	爷爷	221
gray	HUĪSè	灰色	211
green	LùSè	绿色	209
hair	tóUfa*	头发	147, 19
hamburger	HànbǎoBĀO	汉堡包	223
happy	GĀOXìng	高兴	23, 161
has	yǒu	有	177
he	TĀ	他	139
hot dog	Règǒu	热狗	225

ENGLISH	PĪNYĪN	汉字	pages
how	zěnme*	怎么	187, 75
how many?	jǐge*	几个	49, 25
how much/many?	DUŌshǎo	多少	17, 117
I/me	wǒ	我	153
ice cream	BĪNGqílín	冰淇淋	231
if	rúguǒ	如果	115, 31
is at (a place)	Zài	在	185
isn't good	Bùhǎo	不好	1, 35
just	Jiù	就	55
knows	ZHĪdao*	知道	193, 7
likes	xǐHUĀN	喜欢	155, 47
man	náNréN	男人	91, 111
milk	niÚnǎi	牛奶	237
Mom	MĀma*	妈妈	215
moon, month	Yuè	月	183
movie	Diànyǐng	电影	11, 175
name	mínGzi*	名字	85, 199
noodles	Miàntiǎo	面条	227
o'clock	diǎnZHŌNG	点钟	13, 197
orange (color)	chénGSè	橙色	207
orange (fruit)	chénGzi*	橙子	235
peach	táOzi*	桃子	235
person	réN	人	111
pink	fěnhónGSè	粉红色	213
pizza	PĪSà	披萨	223
pork	ZHŪRòu	猪肉	229
purple	zǐSè	紫色	209

ENGLISH	PĪNYĪN	汉字	pages
red	hónGSè	红色	207
rice	mǐFàn	米饭	227
salad	SHĀLĀ	沙拉	225
sandwich	SĀNmínGZhì	三明治	225
says	SHUŌ	说	131
sees/looks	Kàn	看	57
sells	Mài	卖	73
she	TĀ	她	141
sister (older)	jiějie*	姐姐	217
sister (younger)	Mèimei*	妹妹	219
sky	TIĀN	天	143
soup	tánG	汤	237
strawberry	cǎoméI	草莓	233
taco	tǎKĒ	塔科	223
tall	GĀO	高	23
tea	chÁ	茶	237
that (one)	Nàge*	那个	89, 25
therefore	suǒyǐ	所以	137, 169
they	TĀmen*	他们	139, 81
they (female)	TĀmen*	她们	141, 81
this, this one	Zhège*	这个	189, 25
time	shÍhou*	时候	125, 45
today	JĪNTIĀN	今天	53, 143
tofu	Dòufu*	豆腐	231
tomorrow	mínGTIĀN	明天	83, 143
very	hěn	很	41
wants	Yào	要	163

ENGLISH	PĪNYĪN	汉字	pages
wants to/feels like	xiǎng	想	157
watermelon	XĪGUĀ	西瓜	235
we	wǒmen*	我们	153, 81
week	XĪNGQĪ	星期	159, 101
what	shéNme*	什么	121, 75
which	něige*	哪个	87, 25
white	bāISè	白色	211
who	shéI	谁	119
why	WèishéNme*	为什么	149, 121, 75
with, and	GĒN	跟	27
woman	nǔréN	女人	97, 111
year	niáN	年	95
yellow	huáNGSè	黄色	207
you	nǐ	你	93
you all	nǐmen*	你们	93, 81
yummy	hǎoCHĪ	好吃	35, 3

Calendar and Time		
year	年	niáN
month	月	Yuè
week	星期	XĪNGQĪ
today	今天	JĪNTIĀN
tomorrow	明天	mínGTIĀN
Monday	星期一	XĪNGQĪYĪ
Tuesday	星期二	XĪNGQĪÈr
Wednesday	星期三	XĪNGQĪSĀN
Thursday	星期四	XĪNGQĪSì
Friday	星期五	XĪNGQĪwǔ
Saturday	星期六	XĪNGQĪLiù
Sunday	星期天	XĪNGQĪTIĀN
January	一月	YĪYuè
February	二月	ÈrYuè
March	三月	SĀNYuè
April	四月	SìYuè
May	五月	wǔYuè
June	六月	LiùYuè
July	七月	QĪYuè
August	八月	BĀYuè
September	九月	jiǔYuè
October	十月	shÍYuè
November	十一月	shÍYĪYuè
December	十二月	shÍÈrYuè
1:00 (one o'clock)	一点钟	YĪdiǎnZHŌNG
2:00	两点钟	liǎngdiǎnZHŌNG
3:00	三点钟	SĀNdiǎnZHŌNG

Food		
apple	苹果	pínGguǒ
banana	香蕉	XIĀNGJIĀO
beef	牛肉	niÚRòu
chicken (meat)	鸡肉	JĪRòu
chocolate	巧克力	qiǎoKèLì
cola	可乐	kěLè
dumplings	水饺	shuǐjiǎo
hamburger	汉堡包	HànbǎoBĀO
hot dog	热狗	Règǒu
ice cream	冰淇淋	BĪNGqÍlíN
milk	牛奶	niÚnǎi
noodles	面条	MiàntiáO
orange	橙子	chénGzi*
peach	桃子	táOzi*
pizza	披萨	PĪSà
pork	猪肉	ZHŪRòu
rice	米饭	mǐFàn
salad	沙拉	SHĀLĀ
sandwich	三明治	SĀNmínGZhì
soup	汤	tánG
strawberry	草莓	cǎoméI
taco	塔科	tǎKĒ
tea	茶	chÁ
tofu	豆腐	Dòufu*
watermelon	西瓜	XĪGUĀ

244

Family		
family/home	家	JIĀ
dad	爸爸	Bàba*
mom	妈妈	MĀma*
sister (older)	姐姐	jiějie*
sister (younger)	妹咩	Mèimei*
brother (older)	哥哥	GĒge*
brother (younger)	弟弟	Dìdi*
grandma	奶奶	nǎinai*
grandpa	爷爷	yÉye*

Pronouns		
I/me	我	wǒ
you	你	nǐ
she	她	TĀ
he	他	TĀ
we	我们	wǒmen*
you all	你们	nǐmen*
they (female)	她们	TĀmen*
they	他们	TĀmen*

Colors		
red	红色	hónGSè
orange	橙色	chénGSè
yellow	黄色	huánGSè
green	绿色	LùSè
blue	蓝色	lánSè
purple	紫色	zǐSè
gray	灰色	HUĪSè
white	白色	bāISè
black	黑色	HĒISè
pink	粉红色	fěnhónGSè
brown	咖啡色	KĀFĒISè

People		
friend	朋友	pénGyou*
person	人	réN
man	男人	náNréN
woman	女人	nǔréN
Chinese (person)	中国人	ZHŌNGguÓréN
American (person)	美国人	měiguÓréN
girlfriend	女朋友	nǔpénGyou*
boyfriend	男朋友	náNpénGyou*

Color in your dragon's scales as you complete each character picture page.

CPSIA information can be obtained
at www.ICGtesting.com
Printed in the USA
LVHW060502180619
621193LV00008B/11/P